to Olivia.

without you, i wouldn't be here today. you've brought me down from so many cliffs and talked me through so many of my issues. you have stuck by my side for so many years that life without you seems impossible and boring, you make everyday magical and you make the world brighter simply by existing. thank you for being you and never judging me when i make stupid choices. i love you endlessly. you're my best friend always and forever ugly <3

part one:
simply me.

these first few pieces you're about to embark on, simply give you some insight as to who i am.

they come from the deepest parts of my mind and i tried to do my best in encompassing who i am with them but at the end of the day i think i'm far too complex to be put into a few measly words.

i am ethereal and otherworldly.

i am simply too much for the world we live in.

i hope these paint you a better picture.

where i'm from.

i'm from a place where worlds collide,
on the border of charlotte and mint hill is where i reside.
a yellow house with wizards, cat toys, and more cd's and books than can be counted,
on the big tree out front where the flowers bloom in the spring, rests my mothers's many birdhouses.
I happen to know the owners of that quirky little yellow house.
you call them "penny and dennis" but i have the honor of calling them "mom and dad".
momma's always said "God pays back debt without money".
that's always been her way of telling me that those who've wronged me will get what's coming to them, our own special form of karma.
growing up my days were spent between that yellow house and the small tan house next door.
from the small tan house next door i would go to the small elementary school miles down the road.
from that small school i would go to the ymca for afterschool.
from afterschool i would always end up at my best friend's house, which was conveniently six houses from mine.
i'm sad to say that i can no longer remember how we spent our time together.
i can remember that we were rascals growing up and were without a doubt getting into some kind of trouble.
i'm happy to say that even today, fifteen years later, my best friend and i are still getting into trouble.

she no longer lives six houses down from me, but she does live just a few miles down the road with her two kids, and two dogs.
she shaped me into who i am today.
i'm from family dinners at the table for holidays only.
i'm from family night and pizza's every saturday.
i'm from "let's watch a scary movie while mom takes a nap!"
i'm from "amber come watch this lifetime movie with me!"
i'm from watching all my children with my mom every day until the show was canceled.
now i watch bold & the beautiful every chance i get at 1 pm with her.
i'm constantly changing and growing and i can't wait to see where i'll be from five years down the road.

childhood trauma.

i've spent quite a bit of time trying to come to terms with the way my upbringing has been.
as a child, i tried not to think about it too much because i had too much to worry about,
such as, what shenanigans will talia and i be getting up to today?
what snack am i gonna eat after school?
what movie should i watch while i do my homework?
now that i'm older i've tried to understand it.
in case you're new here allow me to break it down.
from the very beginning, i don't think i was wanted.
my mother left me with my grandparents when i was a baby and i was raised by them.
she moved in with my dad and his parents and left me behind.
then she had my sister who was able to live with them and not my grandparents and i.
it took her 2 years to realize she was ready to raise a child.
i don't know if leaving me behind was her idea or my dad's but i know that's where my abandonment issues stem from.
four years after leaving me they had my brother,
who was also kept with them.
i'm not trying to complain,
i had a fantastic upbringing.
i love my grandparents with every atom in my body and i owe so much to them.
i just wish i knew why i was left behind.

i was just a baby i don't think i did anything wrong.
my grandma told me that anytime my mom came over and then left i would stand by the window crying and screaming that i wanted to leave with her.
how could she just abandon me like that?
what did i do?
why didn't dad want me either?
my sister and brother went to the same preschool as me,
at the end of the day we'd all sit outside our classrooms and wait for our parents to get us.
and one day that my sister was there my dad was picking her up,
i was told years later that i said hi to him and stood up thinking he was there for me,
i was told years later that he walked right by me to get to my sister.
i don't think he ever wanted me either.
about a month after my eighth birthday everything i knew changed,
my grandma came into the room where i was watching movies with my friend and eating dinosaur chicken nuggets and turned on the news.
i remember it felt like some sort of weird dream.
there on the tv screen was my mom.
"what's mom doing on tv?", i had asked my grandma, extremely confused.
she told me why and i can't remember if i had cried or not.
i don't think i shed a single tear over my father's death.

why shed a tear over someone you barely knew?
i had seen my fair share of horror movies so i knew what the word murder was and what it had meant,
but when my grandma had told me that my mom had killed my dad it still took a bit to sink in.
i just couldn't see how she could do that.
i couldn't wrap my head around it.
my brother and sister then moved in with my grandparents and i,
and that was the hardest change of my life.
i started suffering from depression around this time too.
i remember the first time i went to visit her.
the jail was doing a family day where you could go down and color and take pictures,
it was surprisingly normal which i think was the intention because it was based on the kids coming to see family.
i still have the picture somewhere.
i didn't see her for a while after that because she was in a maximum security facility and my grandparents didn't want us to see her like that.
she was transferred to a smaller more relaxed facility in troy and that's when we started seeing her more often.
we tried to see her once a month because it was so close.
they had a family day too for good behavior.
once a year they had sort of a barbeque with games and dancing and face painting.
as awkward as that was i enjoyed it.
it seemed like a day in the park with mom.

even if we were never close i think she really tried to make up for it.
it's been fifteen years since it happened and i still don't know why she did it.
i don't really care anymore either.
it's not going to change anything.
she's in asheville now and she's set to come home in december.
it's so insane to think about.
after almost twenty years without her,
she'll be here with us.
she's going to meet my friends and watch scary movies with me.
is it strange that i'm oddly optimistic about this?
am i setting myself up for disappointment?
i hope things are different.

self improvement.

people know me yet they don't know me.
people talk at me yet they won't talk to me.
people see me yet it's like i'm invisible.
people hear me yet it's as if they don't hear me.
people make assumptions about me before they even know me.
why do we do this?
why do we claim to know things that we don't know?
why do we talk without actually saying anything relevant?
why do we see but only what we want to see?
why do we hear without listening?
why do we judge people?
why do we assume things?
why can't we all just realize that we gain absolutely nothing from doing this.
if you don't educate yourself, or you don't see the full picture or you don't hear the full story, you're never going to become a better version of yourself.
you'll never improve.
get to know people, talk to them, listen to them, look at what they want to show you.
look at someone and see them for who they actually are, not who you want them to be!
the world becomes a better place when you get to know people for who they are.

van gough and i.

i've always felt that the way i see things is much different than the way my peers do.
i never realized that maybe other people see the world that way as well until i watched the vincent van gough episode of doctor who.
when vincent is lying in the field with the doctor and amy and explaining the way he sees the night sky,
i think that's when it clicked for me.
i'm not sure if that was historically accurate or if they were trying to make him seem artsier than he was but it worked.
i, too, see the night sky as a deep blue and i see the stars as they twinkle in the sky above us.
i've felt the wind swirl up around me and through my hair chilling my bones.
the world is so majestic and there are so many things that go unnoticed by people simply because they can't properly see it.
van gough, in the episode at least, saw everything the way he painted it—brush strokes and all.
i see the worlds in words.
everything i lay my eyes on—my mind immediately tries to think of ways to write it and capture its essence just right.
it's something i've done for as long as i can remember.
it's also a way to help me remember specific details that i would otherwise miss or forget.

i remember once in seventh grade, my journalism teacher took us all outside to do an activity and then come back to the class and write about it.
since my mind works in words, my piece had intense detail and my teacher read it out to the class.
i remember being so proud of myself for creating something that was good enough to share with the class.
van gough and i are alike in the sense that we see the entire world as our canvas and see things for all that they are.
i wish i could be half the artist he was.

fire.

how peculiar is it that people tell you and expect you to stay calm in the case of a fire?
it's even more peculiar that they tell you not to hide and instead hurry outside.
why should i hurry when i'm being told by everyone else to stay calm?
i'm supposed to remain calm and in an orderly fashion head outside in a single file line with the rest of my classmates.
if everyone is headed out at the same time regardless of how calm we are,
if the building is on fire then we can assume that the integrity of the building is compromised and the weight of everyone moving through the building at the same time could result in it collapsing!
if the integrity of the building is compromised and everyone isn't calm and they're running through that's even worse because people can fall and get trampled.
if the building is on fire then you risk the ceiling collapsing on you and that will only cause more chaos because then you'd be trapped in the building!
there's so many unknown factors with fires it's not safe to stay calm and it's not safe to run in the building so what do they really expect to happen?
with all that in mind, tell me, would you hurry outside or would you just stay inside?

bad versus good.

how is it that i'm a million times better at writing about the bad times than i am the good ones?
i've sat down on numerous occasions and tried to think about how i could make the good days or even a good time flow into a few simple sentences to explain how i feel,
and every time i've had to delete what i've written because i hate it.
i have so many good times i could write about but they don't flow from my mind in such a way that sounds nice.
i think it has to do with the way all my happy memories seem erratic and all over the place whereas all of my sadder memories are constant and have a direct start and end.
the times in my life are easy to pinpoint but my memory always fails me on the details.
i don't think i'd be able to write a single coherent piece on a happy memory unless the end goal was to drive myself insane.
i try to not dwell on the fact that i can't write about happy things,
it's upsetting to think about and i pray that someday i'll be able to make sense of the good times enough to write something for them.
i want to do them justice and i'm worried that i'll disappoint myself.
i know that i'll disappoint myself because i do it all the time.
i do nothing but let myself down and i can't seem to stop it.
it's just one thing after another.

and no matter what i do,
i'm always going to be a failure.

written during coronacation.

as of late i believe that i'm running out of things to write about. i think it has to do with the fact that i'm stuck in my house and i can't go out and experience things which leads to not having a topic to write about.
if i sit down and try to write about a memory they always skew towards you.
most of my favorite memories include you and then i can't seem to write about anything else and i know that sounds silly but it's the truth.
you were my source of happiness for so long and then you left and you took the sun with you and left me with nothing but darkness.
i could sit here and write about you and the sun and the darkness for hours and hours on end but i know that doing that will only lead me back to the place i was in after you left and i can't put myself through that again.
did you notice that even this piece got skewed towards you too?
i didn't even mean for it to happen but somehow you became the topic of this one.
how do you do that?
you sneak into the corners of my brain and then you make your way out unnoticed.
i've been left alone with my thoughts more often than not during this insane lockdown and i've been having so many good days.

you don't creep into my mind as often anymore and i think that's a miracle.
if this lockdown were to have happened anytime within the last year i know i would've been another statistic and not have made it out alive.
my mind would have eaten me up.
how can we live inside the confines of the same four walls for days on end?
humans need interaction.
we crave intimacy.
we need to be around other people and talking on the phone isn't any sort of fix for that.
i try to keep sane by planning adventures for when we get out of this but i fear that won't ever happen.
i've spent the last few days writing the things that come to mind as they appear and it's a fun way to write.
i feel it's a more intimate way of writing.
it lets you look into my mind and see how it works.
can you see the gears turning?
can you follow my train of thought?
have you figured me out?
i like to think that everything i've written has given people some insight into my mind and that maybe everyone who reads this might know me.
at least i'd hope that someone has figured something out.
i hope you come to think of me as a friend.
i like to think that we're friends.
after all, you have seen the deepest parts of my mind.

i think that has to count for something.
i hope this lockdown is treating you well.
stay safe.

phantom pain.

tonight wasn't that bad considering how bad the bad days can get and yet for some reason it almost broke me?
i really almost pulled my knife out and used it for the first time in months because i couldn't think of any other way to process the emotions i've been feeling.
i've been tugging at my hair and picking at my skin to avoid grabbing it.
i know where it is and that doesn't help.
it's less than twenty feet from me and it's like i'm itching for it.
i constantly feel that ache on my legs and the burn that resulted from it and it gets me through the day.
phantom pain.
the pain from something that isn't actually isn't there but feels real.
that's what i have to look forward to because i know that i'm not going to pick it up again because i know that if i do i don't think that i'd be able to set it back down and that's probably one of the scariest realizations i've had.
it's so addicting and it literally overtakes everything.
you can't think about anything else and during the day you're just thinking about the next time you'll be able to do it.
i used to keep rubber bands on my wrists and snap them against my skin when i felt the urge to hurt myself and i was out in public and it worked for a while until it just didn't anymore.

i'd like to believe that i'm stronger than that and i'm able to refrain from hurting myself but sometimes i seriously question that.
sometimes i truly don't know if i'd be able to survive another day without a mark on my skin.

stay or go?

i've been stuck in my head more often than naught,
and when i sit in my head i think a lot of thoughts.
i think about how i've changed in the past year,
and how i've overcome many of my fears.
i never thought i'd be able to trust anyone again,
i'd never be able to let someone under my skin,
but here you are once again my old friend.
it's you and i trying to make sense of this mess,
and i'd like to think that the outcome from all of this will be a success.
it's been a while since i've sat here and bared my heart and soul,
i feel like i'm losing all control.
you and i both know how much i try to avoid letting people in,
i can't let people see what's underneath the smile lines and behind the grin.
all i seem to do is get hurt and i don't know if i'm strong enough to survive that once more,
i'm struggling between wanting more and needing to isolate and i'm simply torn.
i can't justify opening up to someone,
i know there's always the possibility that it will be worth it in the long run.
but why should i wait forever to find one person?
i suppose that in the end that's the goal,

but after so many times of getting burned—i'm left with a heart of charcoal.
i'd like to think that i've still got so much love left to give and i know deep down all i do is get hurt but my heart is simply too big to keep it to myself,
but then again you've never been good at keeping things to yourself.
and at the end of the day you're only an extension of me,
yet whenever you come around i want to flee.
i never want to spend long in your gaze,
after a while it's blocked by the haze.
the haze of depression and self-hatred,
almost as if they were related.
i want to reach out and have someone reaching too,
but nobody ever is and that leaves me oh so blue.
you and i are here again in the dark of night,
having this same age-old fight.

treat me better.

i don't know why i always let my friends walk all over me.
i suppose i do it because i want them to be happy.
or maybe i'm scared they won't like me anymore if i do something wrong.
i think it's because of what happened with you.
my biggest fear is losing people and i don't want to lose any more.
i just don't know how much longer i can put up with this.
it's not fair that i keep getting treated like this.
i don't get it...
am i not good enough?
do i constantly have to change who i am for people?
do i have to become someone new for every relationship i have?
my friends say certain things when i'm around to show they have dominance over me and it hurts.
i don't know if they even realize that they do it.
if they did realize it what they were doing that would hurt even worse.
i don't want to think that they were trying to hurt me.
they're supposed to be my best friend do you know how much that would suck?
i don't want to think that they would ever do something like that but the more i think about our past and how things have unfolded with us i can't help but think that maybe that's the case?

if i did half the things that they did to me they would freak out on me and say that i was being rude and call me names.
i understand that they have issues but so do i.
i don't try to get people to act a certain way around me because of the issues that i have.
you act like someone else that i used to know and sometimes i can't handle that.
i shouldn't have to feel like i'm walking on eggshells with you.
being friends with me isn't even that hard to do,
just talk to me about celebrities, television shows, movies, memes and we'll be good to go.
it's not like i ask for much.
maybe it's the fact that i'm so "simple" that they think they can just walk all over me?
either way it's still wrong and i shouldn't be treated like this.
i just don't want to deal with them for a little while.
as much as we have fun together sometimes you can be really mean to me.
i don't know.
maybe i'm wrong.
maybe this is happening for a reason?
regardless i wish it wasn't.
i wish my friends treated me better.

where do i go from here?

tonight while i was driving i realized that i don't think—at least for the time being—that i would ever take my own life.
things have been so good lately and i know that the crash from this has to be detrimental and i might feel like i'm not going to make it out alive but i know now that the good days will outweigh the bad ones.
tonight was just proof of that.
tonight was the most fun i've had in ages and if i was to take my life who knows how many good days i'd miss out on?
that feeling really does outweigh the bad days for me.
i love being with my friends.
tonight i laughed so hard that my face hurt for hours after i got home.
i haven't felt that kind of joy in months.
it's odd to think about if i'd ever followed through months ago when i had it all planned,
that i wouldn't have gotten to experience that.
i try not to dwell on that too long.
the thoughts of what i would've missed out on.
it leads me to think about the bad times.
i enjoy nights like tonight especially during a time where bad days are frequent.
i think about the good times when i get down and they do help me pull myself out of that weird funk.

i've never been good at making the good days last but i'm an expert at keeping the bad days around longer than they're needed,
i think it's one of my many talents.
i think i also keep them around because the thought of good days usually means that there's at least eight bad ones right around the corner for me.
all i've known for the majority of my life are bad days so when i don't have them i think my body can't cope and everything just sort of shuts down.
it's been an insane road to even get this far and i feel like i've been working towards it my entire life.
i don't think i ever imagined that i'd reach the end of this road and now that i have i feel oddly incomplete,
as if i'm waiting for the next thing.
i don't even know where i'd begin.
where do you go once you've reached the end?

why don't they stay?

how is it that i can never seem to find a guy who wants to date?
everyone i seem to meet is only here for a friends-with-benefits kind of deal.
i despise that and there's literally nothing i want less than that.
it's embarrassing that i haven't had a serious boyfriend.
it's embarrassing that nobody has ever wanted me for more than a night.
why doesn't anyone seem to want me?
is it me?
is it my personality?
is it how i look?
i'm nearly twenty-one and i've yet to know what it's like to have someone care about you in the way a lover should.
i don't know what it's like to have someone look at you like you were their world.
it's embarrassing that as i'm writing this i'm crying.
i think it's me.
i think i'm just defective.
how else would you explain it?
it can't be the guys' fault...
it's every single guy i meet...
that means it has to be me.
i'm the common factor in all of this.

i've accepted that nobody is ever really going to want me and that's just the way it has to be but that doesn't mean it hurts any less.
i know it's pessimistic to think this way but i've tried every dating app there is and i've shot my shot with a few different people and every time it ends up the same way.
they stick around for a while and then when they're tired of me—which will inevitably happen, i'll be left here reeling.
granted i'm not entitled to anyone or having someone stick around but it'd be nice to just have one person stay.
is that too much to ask?
why won't they like me?

mirror mirror on the wall.

i've been comparing myself to everyone again.
i look in the mirror and i find something new to not like about myself.
there's more flab on my stomach today than there was yesterday and jeez has my nose always been this wide?
everyone i know is better looking than me.
i think i'm never going to like what i see staring back at me.
i think i'll always be stuck in this gray space.
it's the only thing i've ever truly known.
it's almost comforting here.
nobody knows you like your own mind!
i've started bottling things up again too because i can't stand having someone worry about me.
things are bad again and it's only a matter of time before i fall off the delicate cliff i've found myself on.
i have one good day and then by nightfall, it's gone.
maybe i just don't deserve good days?
maybe it's karma for something i haven't figured out or something i did in a past life?
i think it's a little messed up how sometimes i can feel okay about myself and then someone can take a picture of me and suddenly i feel a hundred pounds heavier than i am.
maybe if i stop taking pictures of myself and i don't look in the mirror often i won't have this problem?
that shouldn't be too hard, right?

maybe then i could stop comparing myself to them because i won't even know what i look like.

a ramble from 2020.

recently i decided to redownload bumble because we're on lockdown so i figured i'd try to meet new people.
and i matched with a few cool people and had some decent talks but i know that in-person we wouldn't click.
and we didn't!
i planned on telling them that i'd rather stay friends but they haven't talked to me since then.
maybe they noticed it too?
i felt bad saying that because we have a mutual friend but i don't know what happened.
i'm kind of sad about it because we did click on the phone and i know we'd be great friends but something was just missing when i saw them,
i just knew it wasn't something i was willing to pursue which is fine because i'm not required to.
i don't know maybe it's just a sign that i'm not going to find anyone?
they say that we accept the love we think we deserve and i thought that maybe i deserved at least a little bit of love but all i keep getting are deadends and lost connections.
maybe i don't deserve love?
maybe all i deserve are the friends i have and i'm perfectly fine with that,
i think i just mourn the could have been's.
i know we aren't supposed to compare our real life to television but i still do sometimes.

i just want one stupid fairytale ending.
i'm tired of living in this stupid indie horror movie!
i just don't know what i might have done to deserve something so bland as this.
and i don't think i'll ever know.
i think i'm just stuck waiting it out.
granted none of my friends really seem to be having any luck with this stuff either so i shouldn't feel too bad for myself.
i guess sometimes i let things get under my skin and i let it live there until it eats me up.
i do that quite often.
i let things just get under my skin and i let it destroy me.
i know that i need to stop doing it because it will inevitably be my downfall and i need to work on controlling it.
i need to control myself better too because when it gets late at night and my mind is running a thousand miles per hour things hurt so much worse.
i've always been consumed by my feelings for as long as i can remember but recently i've noticed that it's let up and not been near as earth-shattering as it used to be and i'm thankful for that.
i swear i was only three more breakdowns away from not being able to pull myself back.
when you're in that headspace with the shiny blade in your hand and you can't stop crying,
that's when the intrusive thoughts are the worst, at least for me they are.

i've had to stop myself one too many times from hitting an
artery and just being done with everything,
i know how bad that sounds trust me.
i had to live through it.
i haven't been there in a while.
i'm the only one that can talk me down from that cliff because i
never listen to anyone but myself when i get that way and do
you know how fucking hard it is to talk yourself down?
it's nearly impossible.
yet here i am,
despite all of the odds i'm here.
that cliff is somewhere i hope that i never find myself ever
again.

a ramble about high school.

i need to get back to where i was in high school,
not mentally but physically.
i spent most of my high school years in abandoned buildings
and feeling the cold air seep into my bones in the drafty halls.
i miss my nose turning red and my lips turning blue.
there's nothing quite like the way they make me feel.
nothing will ever amount to that and i fear the day i run out of places to explore.
there's something exciting about seeing places that have been forgotten and all that remains is but a shell of what once was.
i think that reminds me of myself,
for the longest time all i was was a shell of who i used to be.
whenever i went to bethel, for some reason, in the gymnasium there were always birds trapped in there.
it used to make me so unbelievably sad.
watching them flutter around the room trying to find a broken window or an open door to go back outside makes my heart ache.
it reminded me of myself.
i used to be desperate to get out of where i was.
i felt trapped.
exploring these buildings were the only thing that made me feel free.
i used to spend hours there because it was the only place that the thoughts in my head seemed to calm down long enough for me to breathe.

i miss how it was in high school...there were no expectations and every day was something new.
i spent so many days after school getting into trouble or simply having fun with my friends.
sometimes i really miss high school.
i miss my friends and i miss my teachers.
i wish i tried harder in school.
i wish i paid more attention and got better grades.
i could be so much more than this.

a ramble about writing.

nothing has ever been easy for me besides writing.
i remember in fourth grade we were given some assignment to write about what the holiday season was like at home or something along those lines.
i remember mine made me emotional because right around that time my mom went to jail and my dad was no longer alive.
i had written about that because i was in fourth grade i didn't know that it was odd to talk about.
writing has been an outlet for me for as long as i can remember.
i used to make up songs about things too but i've grown out of that since.
poetry and rambles are more my style.
i used to use the back pages of my school notebooks to write poems in class and it used to piss my teachers off,
my sixth-grade year, i think one of my teachers told the councilors something because they used to call me into their office and have me talk about my feelings and things like that,
i only went a few times until i told my mom about that and then i never got called in again.
i kind of enjoyed it,
i didn't have any friends at that school.
it was on the other side of town from me.
i spent most of my time with my head in a book or in the library.

the librarians and i, no matter what school i was at, were always my closest friends.
i've always loved libraries.
i've also always gotten along better with adults than people my age anyways.
i think that has to do with being raised by my grandparents.
although once i got to high school i never spent much time in the library,
i would just hang out in the photography classroom with the teacher.
she was so fun and i think she might have actually hated me,
i feel like i annoyed all of my teachers now that i think about it.
i think it's because i never did the work.
that was only because it was never a challenge for me, besides math, always hated it.
my brain works too fast for the work they gave us so i didn't bother since it was too easy.
i'd rather do something more challenging and end up not doing well than to waste my time on worksheets i don't need and ace them.
i used to love having writing prompts in english class because then i could really put my mind to work and create something brand new!
my favorite thing in the world is writing but i don't like being told what i have to write.
that's what made writing prompts the best,

they merely suggest something and give you an example or they give you a starter and you can run off with it.
i used to fill up college-ruled notebooks with short stories and i think i went through at least three of them in the span of a month.
it was childish nonsense but it was all i had.
i'd spend hours upon hours writing and reading.
i get so sucked into a book that i'm basically in the movie.
my teachers used to hate when i read in class because i could never pull myself out from the book in time to get back with the lesson.
i never minded though, i'd much rather be whisked away to forks washington any day of the week.
i hope my poems and rambles draw you in.
i hope they make you feel the way they make me feel.
i hope things come easy to you.

wandering thoughts and a laptop.

every night without fail i always turn my laptop on and off at least three times.
i'll turn it on when i get home and i'll have something typed out within minutes and i'll sit until i think my brain has turned into mush and after that i'll turn it off.
around one every night i'll turn it back and write another five poems before the clock strikes two-thirty and i'll turn it off again.
four in the morning rolls around and just like clockwork i'm rolling over in bed reaching for the computer again.
i find myself incredibly cursed with the need to write constantly.
i can't even get a peaceful night's sleep because my mind is constantly waking me up with topics to write about and it gives me fragments of things to write about.
i wake up with either the opening lines of a poem or an emotion so fierce that i can't fall back asleep until i've poured every bit of my soul into a computer screen.
there've been times where i'll be blissfully asleep and it'll come to me in a dream and i have to wake up immediately and write it down before i forget it.
sometimes they come to me while i'm driving and then i have to repeat it in my head until i get to a safe stop to put it in my notes.

i'm constantly thinking of things to write about and ways to romanticize the smallest things to better portray them in my writing.
i think this has also brought my downfall.
i've learned to romanticize everything in my life so i tend to overanalyze every interaction i have so i read into them and i set myself up for failure.
i'll just sit here on my floor writing about everything until i can no longer stay awake because even now i know that i should be sleeping because i have work in the morning and i'll be there all day.
i spend every waking moment at work basically.
i get no time to myself unless i'm home and it's the early hours of the morning like it is now.
it's three in the morning as i'm sitting here listening to my oldies but goodies playlist and trying to figure out why things are the way that they are.
i wonder why i feel miserable at work or why i've had constant panic attacks there the past few days since being back from the beach.
i wonder why people think it's nice to play games with my emotions.
i wonder why i'm never able to fall asleep.
i wonder why the numbers of likes and comments on my instagram posts mean so much to me.
i wonder why the smell of your cologne still comforts me even when you're not here anymore.
i wonder how i can still smell it.

i wonder why he doesn't talk to me as often anymore.
i wonder why my dreams have taken such a turn.
i wonder if things will be different with us this time around.
i wonder if i turn the computer off this time if i'll actually be able to leave it off.
i wonder if i'll be able to sleep.

caught in the wind.

all these things keep swirling around in my head.
they confuse me.
they taunt me.
the thoughts of used to be's and might have been's.
the thoughts of almost were's and have been's.
nothing i do ever seems to ease these thoughts or rid me of them.
they just stay swirling around in my head like leaves in the wind.
they go faster than the speed of light and it's so hard to keep up with them.
why can't i just be free of them?
these emotions of emptiness and loneliness come creeping in when i'm feeling great and they bring me to my knees.
being weak leads to irrational decisions,
irrational decisions leads to crying,
crying leads to overthinking and doing something i'll regret in the morning.
it never leads to anything good for me.
thinking these thoughts and feeling this way has never lead me to anything good.
they have made me do unspeakable things that have left me with angry white lines on my skin.
i feel like a shell, a broken and hollowed-out shell.
sometimes i play a game with myself to see how long i can act okay and my record is four days!

after four days i usually lock myself in my room and ignore the outside world for as long as i can.
don't ask questions,
don't look over there,
don't wonder why things are the way they are,
keep your head down,
keep to yourself.
that's what i've learned.
never stopping,
never going,
always stuck in that in-between place on autopilot.
onandonandon.
waitingwonderingwishingpleadingbeggingscreaming.
whycantyouseeme?

buildings and words.

she fell in love, though she never intended to.
she fell in love with something unexpected.
not a person, no, how silly would that be?
she fell in love with places and words.
she fell in love with words because you can say the same thing a million different ways and have it have a million different meanings.
she fell in love with places because she could always find beauty in buildings.
she didn't fall in love with the buildings downtown or the ones with the perfectly manicured lawns.
she fell in love with the buildings forgotten by time.
the ones with the busted in windows and glass scattered round all over the floor.
she fell in love with words once spoken by poets and words that spoke of love and realization and discovery.
she fell in love with authors and fictional characters.
she filled her shelves and her mind with these words and books in hopes that they would help her find herself.
she travelled to faraway places in hopes of it helping her find herself in some broken-down building in tennesee and the crows' nest of that treehouse sure did help.
she always saw beauty in broken buildings because they'd been put through hell.
they saw rebellious teens with spray cans tainting their walls with pointless graffiti, no matter how cool it looked, "she

killed me and she'll kill you too", doesn't need to be on the wall at stonewall.
they saw the ever so lonesome person looking for shelter for the night.
they saw curious minds looking for a thrill.
they saw her come and go on so many occasions they lost count.
they saw her writing her heart out on the closet wall back in cottage five.
they saw her words and how they begged for a change.
she begged for forgiveness, hope, freedom and love.
all the things her heart yearned for.
she still writes about all of these things, but she's traded in dusty closets for a journal and a computer.
she can't remember the last time she felt the chill of an empty hallway or the wind whistling in her ears as she looked down at the level below her.
soon she'll have to make her escape to them.
you'd better hope i make it back.

deserving.

all the words in my head are swirling around so fast that i can't grab them and comprehend them before another thought comes flying in.
it seems as if everything i try to do to catch them is pointless.
i can't figure out what i want to do and i spend my days stuck in my head thinking.
thinking that maybe i'm just not good enough?
thinking that maybe i'm not deserving of the things that i want.
it's an odd sort of feeling.
they say that we accept the love that we think we deserve.
if i don't accept any love at all, does that mean that i don't deserve love at all?
or does it mean that nobody could possibly love me?
or does it just mean that i have yet to find someone that i think is worth my time?
the swirling thoughts in my head seem to attack me and break me down more and more each day.
i can't figure out what all of this means.
maybe i just don't deserve anything at all?

yet another ramble.

i think the reason i'm so good at writing is the fact that i have a troubled mind.
most every great writer had either a tragic backstory or some sort of mental illness.
i guess i got lucky with both!
i've always been troubled and i've been writing for as long as i can remember and then once i started having mental issues the writing really took a turn and it was as if i couldn't put the pen down.
i spend a good amount of my time writing.
i'd do it all day if i could.
it's my escape.
my safe haven.
a world where i couldn't write is a world that i don't really want to live in.
it's nice to get all of my thoughts organized out on paper or on a screen.
i hope my writing will have some sort of impact on people.
the things i write about i like to think are relatable.
although a lot of it is about love and loss and if you haven't been in love it might be hard to relate to.
i just hope it helps someone out there.
there are so many thoughts that go through my mind on a daily basis i feel as if i'm suffocating in my head.
writing down the thoughts as soon as i think them helps me feel a little less trapped within the confines of my head.

i ramble a lot and everyone knows it.
it helps to write it all down.
is it bad for me to hope that i never heal from the things that have hurt me because i'm worried that i won't be able to write without the pain?

a full mind.

a mind full of words to say but no way to say them.
a mind bursting with ideas and thoughts but no way to bring them to life.
a mind in constant turmoil over a future she isn't even sure she has.
a mind in a constant battle against itself and the voices inside of her mind.
a mind trying to break free from the constant noise.

she'd never known confusion like this.
she didn't see the point of trying.
she didn't see the point of waking up in the morning.
she just wanted to vanish,
to wither away.

she wanted to go to the abandoned asylum in virginia that she'd read so much about.
she felt like she'd belonged there.
as if it was a lighthouse beacon calling her home.
she can't get the voices in her head to quiet down.
they're yelling so loud that it's deafening.

she's trapped within the confines of her own mind.
how is she meant to escape that?

for sam.

she was like a pool on a hot day.
she was like the moon to the earth.
she was needed by everyone but she never knew it.
she was a story, a tragic one, but a story nonetheless.
people still speak of her, in reminiscence and hushed voices.
a few people know the true story of who she was, those same people were absolutely crushed to find out that her story had ended.
the world without you is a cold and desolate place.
why did you do it?
now you're forever stuck at sixteen and i'm stuck here aging without you.
you were the sister i never had and we were always supposed to have each others backs.
it's not fair, you were supposed to be twenty-six this year and we were supposed to go out on the town.
i never got to see you graduate or how you looked in your prom dress, which we both know you would've looked beautiful in.
it's not fair.
i can still remember the day it all happened with such clarity it's almost as if i'm still there.
i remember the panicked phone call to mom asking her to go to your house to check on you as my bus drove by your ambulance ridden house.
i remember freaking out all day wondering if you were okay.

i remember mom texting me that she wouldn't tell me what happened until i got home.
i remember telling talia i had a bad feeling about it.
did you know she has two kids now, a little girl and boy, you would've loved them?
i remember coming through the door and sitting on my mom's bed and her telling me that it was you who didn't make it.
i remember immediately breaking down right then and there.
i then called your phone, not believing it, i just wanted you to answer the phone.
i needed you to.
after the sixth call and hearing your voice on the voicemail i knew it was true.
i think about you all the time.
i know one day i'll see you again but until then, everything i do is for you.

close enough to hurt me.

lately i've been thinking more about the issues i have.
surprise i have issues!
i've been thinking about my trust issues
i never realized until a few days ago just how serious they were,
i thought i was a bit of an open book but i realize now that a lot of my friends know very top layer stuff about me.
they know the basics but they don't really know what makes me who i am.
i have about three people in my life who know the deep stuff, my hopes and fears and my dreams.
i can't seem to open up because i can't seem to make myself believe that anyone would want to stick around.
i still worry that my three best friends are going to get bored of me one day and leave.
they've been in my life for years but i still worry that they'll just pick up and go leaving me in the dust one day.
i know i shouldn't think this way and i should have more confidence in them but i've only known people to leave me since i was a child and my parents left me.
that's where everything comes from and it didn't help that the cycle continues so often with friends and lovers to the point where i can't tell up from down.
i've been lucky enough to have some friends from work that i've opened up to a little bit but i've been there a year and a half

and i feel like i've barely made progress with opening up to them.
it's so pointless when jobs are just temporary fixtures in our lives and either i'll leave or they will.
nobody stays at one job forever especially a part-time retail job.
i've had too many people come and go that i just don't see the point of letting someone get that close.
i won't let you close enough to hurt me.
being open and vulnerable is terrifying because it's always used against me and i just can't put myself through that again.
sorry if i come off as distant or standoffish i just can't let myself be crushed again by those with ill intentions.
i've built up walls so high that i can no longer see over them.
i can't let you close enough to hurt me.

am i good?

i've spent a good amount of my life belittling myself and tearing myself down.
i could never convince myself that i was worthy of anything deemed as good.
i still have a hard time thinking that.
anytime i have a good day i sit back and i think about what i could've done to deserve it.
how silly is that?
i have to second guess why i'm having a good day.
i guess the years of self-inflicted torment worked.
you say horrible things about yourself but you never stop to think about the consequences down the road.
i can't take a compliment because i've conditioned myself to believe that i'm not attractive ever.
i can't seem to wrap my head around the fact that i am beautiful and that i am deserving of the things that i have go well in my life.
i'm afraid it will always be this circle and i'll never be able to break free from it.
we have to be nicer to ourselves otherwise we'll all end up like me and trust me that's not fun.
it's a daily battle.
i guess maybe i'm not worth a single good day.

adventure.

my heart longs for something new.
it's been far too long since i've done anything fun.
we've been locked up in our houses for far too long and while i'm able to get out of the house for work that does absolutely nothing for the wanderlust i seem to always have.
i think the first place i might go is right back to the mountains.
or maybe i'll find a new abandoned place and place my words on a forgotten wall.
i always like to adventure most when i'm looking for myself and there's nothing i'd want more than to spend time alone in a place forgotten by people.
sadly i'm stuck exploring the well-known aisles of my local pet store.
i sit in my room waiting for the wave of hopelessness that always hits me late at night and pray that it gives me enough motivation to write about the places i've been and the places that i'll go.
there's always something to explore along the blue ridge parkway,
i might have to pay it a visit when this is all over and drive through a few new towns!
the thought of that is enough to push me through the lockdown.
the possibility of abandoned places has always been enough motivation.
hopefully, i'll be able to find something.

i believe in myself.
i think i can pull something out from my sleeve.

bad day.

had my first bad day in a while today.
it's been so long i didn't know how to talk myself down.
i had a few different panic attacks today and i don't know what triggered them or how i even handled them i think i just blacked out.
it's been so long since i've felt like this.
what happened?
i was doing so well?
i also feel like a nuisance to my friends because all i do is post about my writing and i think they're all getting tired of me.
i would be tired of me too.
the guy that i spent a majority of the year on and i've been talking to since november,
or i thought we were talking,
told me today that he wouldn't ask me out because of the distance and i'm the only one who puts effort into it.
which i wasn't expecting because i thought we did a good job at seeing each other and i thought he was into this too.
i admit that it felt like i was the only one putting effort into this long before he mentioned anything about it.
i was always the one messaging first and asking to facetime and asking when he was free so i could come to see him.
i don't know how i didn't see it sooner.
i'm always the last one to notice something and it's one of my worst traits.
i'm always late to the party.

i mean granted i'm good at noticing when things are changing!
i'm just bad at noticing that things were bad from the beginning.
i'm not sure what the point of this piece is.
i suppose it's just a ramble.
needed to get the thoughts out of my head and my fingers were just itching to get on the keyboard.
lately i feel like the only thing that's been keeping me sane is writing something new every night.
it's all i have to look forward to.
is that sad?
i think that might be a little sad.

quiet.

i often think about all the things i should've said.
things that should've slipped past my lips in the heat of the fight.
a comeback that should've been spoken louder so i wouldn't have been standing on the sidelines like a fish out of water.
things that i should've said louder during two am conversations even if you were asleep on the other end of the phone.
i should've said more.
i've said so much during my short period of time on earth but i don't think i've said the things that i've wanted to say nearly as much as i should.
and even if i did say the things that i meant to say i never said half of the things that i should've said to you.
and i think about that all the time.
there's already so much stuff i regret not saying.
so much that i regret not doing.
so many missed opportunities because i've been too quiet.
i need to learn how to say what i feel in the moment.
i've always been the type to shy away from the things i want because i've been too scared to go get what i want.
i need to learn how to take control and do things the way that i want them to be.
i need to stop letting people walk all over me.
it's been a habit that i've had for far too long and i need to break the cycle.

no longer will i sit back and allow myself to be treated like a doormat for other people's enjoyment.

here we go again.

how is it that no matter how many times i think i meet someone who seems different from everyone else they turn around and prove me wrong?
there were two guys recently who i thought were different from all the rest and it's almost as soon as i thought that they switched up.
one of them made me so uncomfortable in my own room,
that's my area,
my safe space.
i can't have bad memories like that in here.
i had to kick him out.
and then someone from high school popped back into my life and i thought that maybe they had changed but it's been two days and i haven't heard from him and he was at his ex-girlfriend's house today.
i suppose that makes sense though because that's how it turned out last time too.
you'd think that four years would make some sort of a difference in a person but maybe i was the only one who used the time to change?
maybe they're content with who they are.
which is fine i just personally wish they'd spent more time on their friends.
most guys think that i'm so very intrigued by the blank and boring selfies that they send every time we "talk".

i'm so very sorry to burst your bubble but there's nothing i hate more than that.
i can't get to know you by the four different ways you take selfies.
i don't know what you expected from that.
i much prefer texting to snapchat mainly because of that.
there's so much a text can say but the dumb pictures they send only mean one or two things.
more often than not they're just trying to get in my pants and i'm not the type to give in easily to that kind of stuff.
i think i've already met my soulmate and we just need time to work on ourselves,
they say by the time you're in your twenties you've already met them.
i'd like to think i met mine already but there's also a part that dreads that.
none of the guys in my life are really "soulmate" worthy if you know what i mean.
they're all mostly frat boy types.
and i don't know about you but i'd rather not be stuck with a chad for the rest of my life.

part two:
you.

i write a lot about a "you" and for the most part they're all the same person. other times they're about someone else and every once in a while they're the idea of someone.

the "you" i write about most, however, is the first guy i've ever loved, he didn't love me back and that honestly tore me up more than i'd care to admit.

i never once for a second doubted that i loved him though because i know what my feelings are and i know that i've never felt that with anyone, before or after him, and learning how to adapt to life without him is something i wouldn't wish on anyone.

i've done a lot of writing about you. i hope maybe one day you'll read it. i do miss you.

natural.

i remember our first kiss often.
it was as easy as breathing, even if it took me a year and a half to actually do it.
we were at your house on the couch watching power rangers because you were adamant that i watch it.
it started out as a shy, innocent thing.
every thought in my head flew out, the only one remaining was "why didn't i do this sooner?", the second your lips touched mine.
it was the most natural thing i'd ever done.
as it got more heated you were on top of me with your hands slowly making their way up my shirt, your fingertips ghosting along my skin.
i remember thinking it was a dream and trying to get myself to wake up.
this wasn't the first time your hands had made their way against my skin but it was the first time it'd felt so real.
this wasn't late at night in the car, this was during the middle of the day and it made everything electric.
kissing you was as easy as saying my own name.
i asked you a million times if you were comfortable with what was happening because i know you're always a little iffy when it came to physical stuff.
we'd always texted things but rarely physically did them.
it only seemed natural to ask how you were doing during it all.

after our, in my opinion, short-lived makeout we cuddled on the couch and i almost fell asleep.
soon after you drove us to the park to meet up with some people you knew and family and we listened to music and sang along horribly off-key just for the laughs.
i met people that you'd known all of your life and the family members you'd told me stories about on holidays.
your aunt and uncle gave you money for snow cones and you told me that everyone who was meeting me really liked me and that made my heart soar,
being accepted by those closest to you had to be a good sign for us, right?
you made a joke about how you bring someone new every year and i remember thinking to myself that i'd be here every year just because that's just how things turned out with us.
somehow you convinced me to play soccer with you, which was met with "i played softball instead for a reason!" and that reason was quite a good one.
you hit me in the face with the ball more than once, i still don't know how that happened.
the sight of you throwing your head back with your nose crinkling from laughing will always be one of my favorites.
you ran over and picked me up in your arms as if it was your natural reaction and we did it all the time.
you kissed the top of my head and apologized for doing it, which you didn't have to do because it was an accident but i appreciated it nonetheless.

that day will always live in my memory as one of the best days of my life.
i wouldn't trade that for anything.

center part I.

as i lie there under the covers tracing my fingers along his spine as he sleeps peacefully beside me, i start to think of all the things that could be.
the things that may happen if we continue like this.
if we continue on the road we're on, will we crash and burn?
will we be fine and never worry about the repercussions?

as i lie there breathing in his cologne and thinking, my mind starts to wander.
to what it'd be like to fall asleep and wake up next to him every morning.
to fall into his arms when i can't take the weight on my shoulders anymore.
to fall onto the couch next to him and watch a whole season of doctor who in one day with him.
to fall in love with the boy with the beautiful blue-green eyes that i seem to drown in every time they look in mine.
as i press my lips to the soft skin of his neck i begin to wonder what it'd be like to be able to kiss him whenever i wanted to.
not in the secrecy of a house where walls don't talk.

i want to feel his lips brush against mine as he holds me and we talk.
i want to be able to call him mine and hold his hand.
i want to be with him in every way imaginable for the rest of my life.

as i lie there with my legs intertwined with his i laugh to myself and can't help but think of how it reminds me of us and how we're intertwined.
intertwined by the marks left where wandering eyes can't see.
intertwined by phone calls we'll never repeat.
intertwined by shy glances across the room.
intertwined by sweet nothings whispered in our ears.

as i lie there hearing him speak in hushed tones, i think about what it'd be like to hear him all the time.
i'd like to hear him in the morning when his voice is still rough with sleep.
i'd like to hear him right before bed when his words would slur together from being half awake.
i'd like to hear him sing until he lost his voice at a concert with me or singing so loud in the car that we can't hear the wind rushing past our ears.
as i run my fingers down his jaw feeling the stubble starting to grow back, i smile because of the contrast of his rough face to my smooth fingertips reminds me of us.
him: a hands-on, loud-mouthed barbarian.
me: a quiet, keep your head down, fragile thing.
how we're from two different worlds yet here we lie in the same bed.

i find myself twisting my fingers around his hair as the knots in my stomach become more apparent from overthinking.

i'm overthinking everything, possible outcomes, knowing he and i will never be and nothing good could come from this. i'm holding him like it's the last time i'll see him because i know that when i get home he'll already be forgetting me until the next time he needs me.

he will never know that he has become the center of my thoughts.
he will never know that he has become the center of my dreams.
he will never know that he has become the center of my nightmares.
he will never know that he has become all i can write about.
he'll never know.

stonewall.

the sound of ice and snow crunching under our feet side by side.
along the desolate road are rows and rows of buildings forgotten by time.
swirling in the air above us are clouds of our breath.
we continue our walk down the pavement with toes going numb in our shoes and our noses redder than rudolph.
to our left sits a pile of snow, despite the below-freezing temperature outside we grab handfuls of snow and fling them at one another.
when we can no longer feel our fingertips we call a truce and continue on our way.
the only sounds besides our voices are owls and water dripping from icicles.
we cross over the vine-covered icy bridge slipping over the icy leaves and fall on our backs one too many times.
we walk up the small path to the chapel across the street and make our way inside.
graffiti covers all of the remaining pews and despite it being pitch black i can tell that you look astonished.
our eyes slowly adjust over the span of the hours we're there and i can see you clearly now.
despite being red from the cold, you're still the most beautiful thing i'd ever laid my eyes on.
we sit on the stage isolated from the outside world and talk about our hopes and dreams.

the sounds of our laughs ricocheting around the small building
filling it with joy,
our cheeks hurting from it all.
i'd never seen you so happy.
if only i had told you how i felt that night,
maybe things would be different now.

parking lots.

the parking lot between panera and target will always hold a spot in my heart.
the middle section two to four spots back.
that will always be our spot.
it's where we hung out for the first time and where you really let me into the darkest parts of your mind.
"contact solution" will always be our little inside joke.
after a hard night at work that's where you could find us.
it's where we would sit for hours on end until my dad would call me asking to come home.
it's where hands slid under shirts and inhibitions were lost.
it's where lips met skin and i first realized that there might be some potential between us.
it took me a little over a year and a half to work up the courage to kiss you and when i did i realized that i didn't want to kiss anyone else ever again.
i sit in our spot sometimes and i think about you, as i so often do, and the memories we made there.
it makes me miss you.
i still see us there sometimes when i close my eyes.
i can see me laughing and doing anything i could to get you to laugh.
i always loved your laugh, it was my favorite sound.
and seeing you smile was something i cherished.
your eyes lit up and sometimes if you thought something was really funny you'd throw your head back as you laughed.

i could sit and look at you for hours.
you were my favorite person in the universe and i wished i could live in your gaze forever.
you were my sun,
but to you i was in another galaxy.

you part I.

a lot of what i write about is sad and depressing,
i can't help it though that's just how my mind works.
though whenever you come around it's as if the sun has broken through the clouds and i can finally breathe.
with one blink of those lovely eyes that seem to see right into my soul,
i feel freer than i have in my entire life.
we have so many wonderful memories together,
driving to who knows where in my car that rainy afternoon when we left during the intermission of our school's latest play.
playing games in target almost every day after school.
spending hours upon hours driving around to find a new place to explore.
all these memories have one thing in common.
they all have you.

you part II.

late at night when i can't sleep, you're on my mind.
when i feel like i can't hold back the floodgates anymore, you're the first person i reach out to.
when i need to have a laugh after a hard day, i know i can count on you.
when i need to rant to someone, i know you'll be right there waiting.
i know it will never be the same for you.
i know i'm never on your mind.
i'm nothing but a fleeting thought.
a footnote at the bottom of the page.

beauty.

i often find myself thinking about you more and more as the days pass me by.
i sit in my room on the floor and i stare at the words on the wall as my mind drifts to you once again.
how do you do that?
how do you manage to crawl into every corner of my life and seem to live there?
i find myself at a loss for words.
i find myself unable to convert the way i feel about you and the way i see you into coherent sentences.
it's damn near maddening how my words effortlessly fail me when it comes to you.
i'm always so good with the things i say and getting my point across.
words have always been something i've been good with and talking is one of my greatest strengths.
i can never find the right words to say in just the correct order, or i can never find the perfect words to encompass all that you are.
i can never begin to describe you.
thinking of the way your eyes twinkle and your nose crinkles when you smile makes me seem to lose track of time and my train of thought all at the same time.
whenever you laugh every word i've ever learned becomes a useless word scramble that i'd never be able to win.

why must you take away my ability to think clearly?
why can't i speak around you?
i find myself utterly unable to convert your beauty into a single sentence.

friends.

you told me that you needed me today.
i didn't know what to do or how to properly react to that.
i stared at my phone wondering how i got into this position.
after saying for so long that i'd never have a friend with benefits situation and you said that as well,
that seems to be all we are as of late.
for some reason, i come running anytime you call me.
i crave your attention and your touch.
i know that if i were to text you out of the blue as you do to me,
you wouldn't come running.
i don't think you would ever show up.
it's always all give and no take.
i get nothing in return outside of the obvious physical aspect.
are we even friends anymore?
we don't act like it.
i can't remember the last time we hung out where it didn't escalate and if i'm being honest i'm getting tired of this.
even if i'm just a toy to you,
i know that i'll always stick around because i'm just such a fool for you.

part three:
after you.

in this section, you'll be brought to where i was after he left.

the state of mind i was in after he left was worse than dying. i don't know if it was because of where i was in my life when he left or because i had lost someone who i figured would be there until the end.

i'm never going to get that answer and so i'll sit on my floor and write about him until my fingers go numb.

center part II.

it's been a while since we last talked and i know that nobody is to blame but myself.
it's always my fault isn't it?
we've been walking down this lonely road for far too long and my feet are blistered and bleeding.
i think i see the end of the road up ahead and it looks like hell at the end of it.

i'd be lying if i said i wasn't scared.
we've reached the end and i was right.
it's hell on earth here.
you're not here.
where did you go?
it wasn't what i wanted but maybe this was how you always wanted it to end?
traveling down this bitter cold road alone with my arms wrapped around me so tightly that i'm holding myself together.

i think all of the strings inside of me have finally snapped.
what am i supposed to do now?
i'm a doll without any stitches.
i'm falling apart right before your eyes.
why don't you care?
i want you to care.
i need you to care.

it feels like the weight of everything i've ever done is weighing me down and i'm drowning in an abyss in the bottom of the ocean.
this isn't what i wanted.

i wanted you here with me..
i wanted you holding me so tightly that the strings inside of me wouldn't ever dare break.
i'm sorry that everything has fallen apart.
i'm sorry that i seemed to have ruined everything again.
i'm sorry that i'm only capable of making messes.
i'm sorry that every time i seem to close my eyes all i can see is you.
i'm sorry that you seemed to have crawled inside my head and you won't leave.
i'm sorry that you're still the center of my universe.

you part III.

you're constantly on my mind,
no matter how much i try to think about literally anything else,
i seem to fail horribly.
it's impossible to do anything and do it well.
i can't study,
i can't eat,
i can't sleep,
i can barely even breathe.
when everything in my mind is trying to remind me of you.
why do i do that to myself?
i know thinking of you only upsets me and yet there's nothing i can do to stop it.
then my mind is reminding me of our "what-ifs".
all of the things that i'd change,
tiny details that i'd fix,
small things that nobody would ever notice got changed.
the minor things that i'd do to change the events of us.
maybe then things would be different.
maybe you'd feel the same way about me and i wouldn't be stuck here thinking about you when i know you're not doing the same.
maybe then we'd be together and the what if's would go away.

confidant.

i accepted you for all that you were,
your flaws and imperfections and the demons screaming so loud in your head that you couldn't think.
i held you when you were down and i celebrated you when you were strong.
i would drop anything i was doing in the blink of an eye if you needed me.
and i did, on multiple occasions.
i was there through every low and every high.
i helped you through everything.
i confided in you and you in me.
i gave you all of me and you gave me all of you.
everything was always stop and go with us.
you took advantage of my kindness for over two years and i just let you because i thought it was helping.
i never realized at the time that the more i gave to you the less i had of myself.
i lost myself in you and when you decided i wasn't enough anymore i didn't know who i was.
i suffer every day without you...
how could you just leave me like that?
i'm still trying to find myself again.
i don't want to lose the parts of you that i adapted.
i miss you so much it isn't fair.
i hope whoever took my place does right by you.
you deserve the best.

fairytale ending.

i'd like to think that you and i were a "right place, wrong time" kind of thing.
i know that's wishful thinking and i know that you're not coming back and i've come to terms with that but it doesn't help the thoughts from creeping in once in a while.
we had such an insane connection and i know you felt it too.
you can't sit here and deny that to my face because your words always said otherwise.
from the day we met, i was drawn to you like a moth to a flame.
it's odd just how fast i fell for you.
i know what i felt was love and i've never felt that with anyone like that.
i love my friends and my family but it was different with you.
i know you didn't love me in that sense and i know you never will but it was like a drug.
being around you was my fix and i itched when you were gone.
i don't know if i'll ever feel that way again.
i remember the day i realized that i loved you.
it was a scary realization and i knew i couldn't even tell you that i loved you like that.
they make movies about falling in love with your best friend, they write books about it too.
they always live happily ever after.
life isn't a book or a movie though.

why couldn't they make something realistic?
what happens when your best friend doesn't feel the same?
it's hell on earth.
it's the absolute worst feeling.
i hate that feeling.
i hope at some point down the road we'll reconcile and talk things out.
i hope i can get that fairytale ending someday.

what's the point?

it's quite obvious to me now that you don't care nearly half as much as you say you do.
it's taken me this long to see through the veil and come to my senses.
i'll tell you about how i miss you and how much you mean to me, and you'll spill the same thing from your lips but tweak it so it sounds original.
and i fall for it.
every time.
not anymore.
i thought i cared too much about you to let you go, how silly of me.
i still wait for your name to pop up on my phone in hopes that maybe you'd get your act together and tell me how you really feel.
i hate this game that we're playing.
since you don't care about me i wish you'd just tell me and rip the band-aid off.
just give it up.
if you keep playing these games, we're both going to lose.

secrets.

they say that knowledge is power.
i believe that's somehow true.
if you know something about someone, regardless of it being good or bad, you have some sort of power over them.
if you wanted to you could hold that over their head and use it to your advantage.
it's whether you use that information to blackmail them that decides what kind of person you are.
when you trust someone with something about you,
you don't expect them to ever use it against you but sadly that happens more often than you would think.
you hope they'll respect the secrets that slip through your lips at two in the morning and keep it to themself.
ever since meeting you, i've learned many things,
you've taught me more than i'd ever want to know and for that, i have to thank you.
i'm my own person and i deserve more than you'd ever be able to give me.
telling people things that you're ashamed of is terrifying i'd never been so scared to look at my friends.
looking at their faces after i had told them what had transpired between us is probably going to stay with me forever.
they weren't mad at me but they were mad at the situation and at you.
i've never seen olivia that angry and honestly, i'd rather not see her that angry for the rest of my life.

you don't think your actions or words have an effect on people but they do.
nothing you can say or do will ever make me forgive you.
i've given up.
congratulations.
you've won.
you broke me!
your prize is losing a bunch of amazing people who would go through hell and back for the people they love.
you couldn't have asked for a better group of people.
i'm too nice to you.
i'm sorry i got too "clingy",
i'm sorry i was annoying.
i know it's obnoxious and you're not the first person to tell me that.
i'm terrified of what you did happening to me again,
i built up walls so damn high i can't even see over them anymore.
you took the knowledge i gave you and somehow managed to ruin me with it.
are you proud of yourself?
they say knowledge is power and i know too much about you.
i'd suggest watching your back if i were you.

pictures.

the hardest part—for me at least,
is knowing that i have to delete the pictures.
to me, it seems like that's putting a lock on the story of us and throwing away the key.
i don't know how i'm expected to be strong enough to do that.
i look at the pictures more than i care to admit and i listen to the videos often.
even now your voice still soothes me.
looking at them hurts like hell sometimes but for some reason,
i can't tear my eyes away from the screen.
i know i have to delete them in order to move on properly.
they're all snapshots of a better time with you,
but at the end of the day that's all i have.
the idea of you and who i wanted you to be.
they don't show the ugly side of things with us.
i can't keep trying to hold onto that and ignore all of the bad things that you put me through.
i was an entirely different person FOR you.
i became a person who i thought you needed me to be.
i took all of your burdens and your hurt and i made it all my own.
i did so much behind the scenes to help you.
i orchestrated dinners with our friends,
movie nights,
small hangouts outside of work.

i did so much because i couldn't bear to see you suffering like you were.
you never noticed.
you never let me talk to you about my issues because they were "too much" and i seem to constantly ignore that because i held you on a pedestal.
i fell in love with the good, the bad, and the ugly sides of you and you still couldn't come around to the idea of me.
these pictures are all i have of you and i'm too scared to delete them.
you haven't been in my life in two years but somehow this is too hard?
it's the nail in the coffin.
i'm worried that if i get rid of everything i'll forget you.
i'll forget your eyes and how they shine when you smile.
i'll forget your voice.
i'll forget the way you smile and how every single one meant something different.
i'll forget the looks you used to give me from across the room that only made sense to me.
i'll forget you.
it'll all fade away.
i don't want you to become a memory.
you already are.
i don't want to lose you again.
that's what this feels like.
somehow i'm losing you again.
i don't think i'm strong enough to do this.

turned tables.

maybe our entire relationship was a horrible mess that could only crash and burn...
i can't see us being friends anymore.
you've changed and you spent so long without me that i don't have a part in your life anymore.
i grew out of the mold that you made me fit into.
did you even know you did that?
you do it to everyone,
you change them slowly to fit this mold of how you want them to be and it's so gradual that the person doesn't even know it's happening.
it doesn't seem right for us to continue whatever we are.
you won't care though because your life revolves around her and i'm not her.
when she decided that you could be in her life and then she proceeded to treat you how you're treating me,
you lost it.
you spent so many nights talking bad about her and venting to me about how you were conflicted about her,
and then you treat me like that and just expect it to be okay?
you've always used my feelings for you to your advantage.
you knew how to manipulate me and you did it so perfectly.
you don't care about me though or how those actions affect me because i'm simply not her.
i know how long two years with or without someone is.

i also know that at one point you always expected to see me by your side.
do you still feel that way?
i'm not so sure i want to be by your side anymore.
do you have any idea how difficult this is for me?
you're my best friend.
you're all i had.
i figured you and i had a forever kind of relationship.
and now i have to rethink everything i've ever known about you because you decided to push me to the side as if i'm nothing to you.
i'm not sure if i can even talk to you,
all you do is avoid me.
i get opened messages and blank stares.
i'm getting another job soon and then we won't even see each other.
you always used to try and guilt me into staying there because you couldn't handle the job without me.
it was you and i against everyone else, do you remember when you said that?
do you remember anything?
i'm debating just blocking you to just get it over with.
you're dragging it out and it's killing me.
isn't that funny?
you usually always block me,
but i guess this time i'm gonna be the one to pull the trigger.
it's funny how the tables turn.

two am decisions.

she often found herself sending texts at two in the morning.
she sent texts to boys who would never feel anything other than lust towards her.
she knows they'd never need anything more from her yet she couldn't seem to stop herself from sending out those fatal messages.
she supposed she sent them to try and fill the void in her heart left by past lovers who had done her wrong.
although she never really enjoyed the acts that followed as much as she acted like she did.
she figured it was better than another night alone with that same ache in her chest.
being used time after time seems to lose its effect after a while and suddenly she's right back where she started.
she's going through the motions and blocks it out until it's over and she blindly reaches for the discarded clothes on the floor.
and now she's searching for her keys and walking towards the door thinking how stupid of a decision it was to show up in the first place.
she knows it wasn't the right decision but she knows that within the next week she'd be right back in his bed after sending those stupid two in the morning messages.

senses.

it's been a little over an hour since we said our goodbyes.
i can still feel your hands on me.
i can still smell the stench of stale cigarettes on my clothes and i can still taste them leftover from your lips on mine.
i can still hear you whispering into my ear and i can feel your lips against my skin.
i can feel your lips on my neck and i can feel your teeth sinking into my palm and my cheek.
your hands were grabbing whatever flesh they could get and holding tight as if your life depended on it.
it's been three days now and your mark is still on my neck and your fingertips are still marked on my hips.
you marked me so easily even though i said not to.
why didn't you just listen?
now i'm stuck with the burning reminders of the mistakes we've made and i don't know how long it will take to fade.
i can feel the shame burning in my veins and it doesn't help that i have to see you every day.
it's been a week now and i've, for some unknown reason, decided that i was going to meet you again and repeat this ridiculous cycle.
this time your hands found their way around my throat and i thought for sure it was going to be over for me,
my vision was fading and it took tugging harshly on your hair for you to snap out of it.
i left shortly after that.

it's been a day and a half and my head feels heavy.
it's been a week and my neck still aches.
i've come to my senses and i've decided that you're never going to lay your hands on me ever again.
i never want to taste your nasty cigarette flavored lips and i never want to come home smelling like them.
i never want your teeth to touch my flesh.
i want you to stay far away from me.

destruction.

destruction is everywhere.
everyone, at some point in their lives, will cause some sort of destruction.
it's not something you can escape or avoid.
it'll grab you by the hair and drag you through the mud time and time again.
taking something that was once beautiful and then turning it into something broken.
what a sad thought it is that not only does this work for objects but it also works for people.
you could meet the most optimistic person and turn them into a pessimistic broken mess.
you can twist and mold them into anything you want just like putty in your hands.
you take paint and color beautiful pictures on broken and cracked walls,
that's creating beauty in the midst of destruction.
that's what we try to do right?
try to make something lovely out of something broken?
that's what i've tried to do,
it's why i write.
i try to make something nice out of all the hurt.
it makes me feel better.
you can destroy someone without even realizing it.
words can hurt, thoughts can too.

everyone has the ability to destroy, and everyone has the ability to create something lovely instead.
make sure you make the right choice.

1:30 with you.

it's like one thirty in the morning.
all i can think about are all the one thirties we've spent together.
it's been a while since we've both been asleep by now.
we've spent so many nights talking.
now all i can think about is all of the one thirties we've missed.
do you miss me?
i miss you something fierce.
i wanted to spend every moment of my life in your presence and i know that you'll never reciprocate that.
i think you're never going to talk to me at one thirty ever again.
you're getting used to life without me and soon you won't even need me.
if you get used to life without me why would you ever want to phase me back in?
you got so used to life without me that it slowly became your new "normal",
why would you need me anymore,
i was just another pitstop on the road to you.
soon i'll be nothing more than a distant memory in your mind that you think of once in a blue moon.
i hope that you think of me often.
i hope you end up happy.
i miss one thirty with you.

new years with you.

sometimes i wish it were new years again.
everything was so simple at the beginning of this year.
you came down to see me and spend new years with me.
you stopped by my job and you met the people in my life and that made my heart soar.
i've never had a guy want to meet my friends and the people close to me,
made me happy.
while we were watching a movie you phone kept going off and i asked you about it because i was trying to enjoy the masterpiece that is Prisoner of Azkaban.
you told me it was your friends asking you to come over to a party.
i told you that you should go,
it'd been a while since you saw them and who am i to hold you from your friends?
you were shocked that i let you go.
you told me that your ex never would've let you go.
i told you that i'm not your ex and as long as i got to see you the next day before i went to work i wouldn't care.
i had one request though.
i wanted my new years kiss before you left.
"kiss me like you mean it", is something that i always said to you.
it was our thing.

i grabbed you by the front of your shirt and kissed you and then sent you off to meet your friends.
told you to text me when you got there but you called me while you drove because you knew i'd miss you.
and i did.
as soon as you left i missed you.
i texted you all night but i still let you have fun.
you showed up the next morning around eight-thirty.
i woke up sick as a dog.
i was shaking but i also felt like i was on fire.
you got into bed with me and made me feel loved even if i looked like death.
i was a sweating mess but you didn't complain at all.
you just laid there and held me as i drifted in and out of sleep.
you fell asleep again eventually and when we woke up we watched some tv and then i had to get ready for work.
i would've called out if i didn't cover someone's shift.
i never told you how much it meant to me that you came back and stayed with me while i was sick.
nobody had ever done that for me.
even if i was sick,
i still miss that time.
now we barely talk and your silence is deafening.
i miss you.
i really do.
i know you think that i don't miss you but after months of being in your life and you in mine...it's hard to not miss you.
i miss new years with you.

__thinking about you.__

i've thought more about you tonight than i have in months.
i wish i knew why you crawled into my mind like you do.
i've heard that if you're thinking about someone that means they're thinking of you too.
or is it if you're dreaming of someone they're thinking of you?
either way i hope i'm on your mind.
it's three in the morning so i guess it makes a little sense why i'm thinking about you,
we always did our best work after one.
why can't you leave me be?
you're not even in my life but you're all over the place.
it's unfair that you got to move on but i'm stuck here with the memories.
take them.
i don't want them or your ghost.
maybe i deserve this?
don't know how i would i was always good to you.
i was yours.
i don't know how i lasted this long.
i should've slipped into madness long ago.
leave me be.
let
me
rest.
i can't stop thinking about you.

january 22 2019.

i think about the last time we saw each other all the time.
it was for the panic! at the disco show.
one of the strangest nights in my life.
it was supposed to be such a fun night but i could clearly tell from the moment i showed up at your house that you weren't all that interested in going anymore.
it was painfully obvious when we were in the arena and i could tell that you'd rather be sat next to anyone else.
when did we become strangers?
when did the air between us feel so thick you could cut it with a knife?
the arena suddenly felt so small.
i would've rather been anywhere else after that.
it was like i didn't know you anymore.
the energy of the crowd was electric from the second the lights turned off but for us it was somehow worse.
i've never felt so uncomfortable next to you.
i'd always been nervous to make a wrong move around you, but this felt like i was walking on broken eggshells and finally messed up.
i knew there was no way to recover from that.
after the show, i saw tyler and i have never been so thankful for a familiar face in my life.
he'd always been a jokester so he, gracefully, brought some ease to my mind.
i remember the drive back to your place was awkward.

i tried to ease it by asking for you to put the radio on.
we got back to your house and i got out of your car and walked over to your door and waited for you to open it.
i knew that we were done, i still held out hope for another month or so though, foolishly.
i gave you one last hug, knowing that i'd never hug you again, and i told you that i loved you.
you didn't say it back, you hardly ever did.
you drove down your driveway leaving me in the road against my car.
i stood there against the small red car, the wind blowing through my hair, and i stood there thinking about the past two years with you.
i made it home shortly after that and sent you a message thanking you for coming and letting you know i'd made it home safely and that was it.
the end of an era.
you and i were done just like that.
the iconic duo who was always by each others sides would now be a separate thing.
amber and adison were no more.
i don't miss you much anymore.
i hurt for so long over this,
i finally am starting to feel like myself again.
i hope you're doing well too.

realize.

what i fail to realize,
as you grab my hand and guide me through the dark and quiet house,
is that you have no intention of keeping me.

you stumble around looking for something to start a fire to keep us warm.
i stand in front of the fireplace in awe of the bumpy map of the mountains that sits framed above the mantle,
as i run my fingers over the texture you call my name.
you needed me to stand over you and shine a light,
that reminds me of all the times i've helped my handyman dad fix things and i smile.
as you continue your frivolous search for the matches the cold air seeps into my bones making me shiver.
the sound of the rain falling around us is oddly calming even if it's the middle of a brutal thunderstorm.
you strike a match and pray that it stays as you hold the orange flame to the papers.
i watch the flame lick its way down to your fingers as i hear you curse and drop the now burnt-out stick and try again.
the rain is coming down the chimney killing the flames before they have a chance to ignite,
much like how we are.

i hear the match strike the box and watch as you try again and your luck has improved because the fire blazes to life.
i watch the small but mighty flame overtake the papers and watch as it grows.
i look to my right and realize you've left my side.
i turn around and find you on the small bed that takes up most of the room.
i walk to you quietly and upon my legs hitting the bed i comment on how it looks comfortable.
i slowly slide onto it and notice that it is nice despite the circumstances.
i lay my head on your chest and rant about work for a moment before trying to hold your hand.
you had other intentions for me as you grab my hand and bring it elsewhere.
from that small gesture, the entire mood in the small room has changed.
the air is so thick i could cut it with a knife and i know that this is my own doing because you've begun to expect things from the late-night messages and pictures.

you don't care much for me and my thoughts as you continue to move me around at your whim.
i feel like a ragdoll, "is it supposed to feel like that"?
you don't seem so harsh in this lighting though if i'm being honest with you.
the way the orange light from the fire is casting onto your skin is almost beautiful.

the way you act now is different from how you used to be though.
i'm used to harsh words and snide remarks which makes me wonder how i even ended up here,
you've always been so rude to me but here i am lying under you as you caress my skin.
i think i just wanted someone easy and you always seemed like such an easy candidate,
you always did have a reputation and you're just upholding it.

i failed to realize something else that night,
you had no intentions of keeping me,
but baby i never had any intentions of keeping you either.

signs.

as i lie in bed thinking about our last few months together i realized that there were so many signs that you were trying to get rid of me.
september wasn't good to either of us and you were a lot more reliant on me than usual because of everything you had going on with her.

october was when we flourished it'd been a while since everything with us moved so smoothly, i truly thought that given a little more time and you would've been mine...that's how good it was to us.
november came and suddenly the messages became less frequent and i saw you less and less, i remember how shitty you had made me feel that month, you were breaking my heart.
i sent you so many messages begging you to talk to me.
i thought that something was seriously wrong and you were pushing the people you were closest to away.
i just needed to know you were okay and you never gave me that peace of mind.

i remember walking through the vineyard towards your host stand, i don't think you knew i was in there, and you were talking to our friend and i heard you say "i think she's finally getting the hint." and you looked over and saw me standing there.

i don't know if you were talking about me but it's the only thing that makes sense.
i remember feeling my heart drop into my stomach.

my worst fears were being confirmed in that sentence.

december came around and by the end of it you had hardly said more than ten words to me but when i came to visit work after i quit, i saw you and i gave you a hug and it was the most awkward hug we'd ever had and i should've realized sooner that you were done with me because looking back now i looked like a fool.
january hit and we were forced to go to that godforsaken concert together and you were a stranger again. we sat in silence and i swear my world stopped spinning.
there were so many missed signs.
you gave me everything i needed to know in the span of those months and i ignored every single one of them…

how could i be so stupid?
i'd always had a fear of you leaving me because i wasn't sure i could handle it, and then you did leave and i couldn't handle it.
i cried for so long over you.
i think the only signs i'd be able to see are the big neon signs.
can we go back and do it again?
i promise i won't ignore the signs this time.
come back.

3:32 am.

some nights the ache in my heart gets so bad that i can't breathe and i have to lay on the floor and spend a while focused on trying to get air to my lungs.
i haven't felt that bad in a while and i'm glad that i'm doing so well i just wish i knew when that change happened.
i like knowing what's going on in my head but lately, i feel like a stranger in my own mind.
i used to have a problem with feeling like i was on autopilot, just going through the motions and never really living.
i used to picture myself floating above my body.
now i feel grounded and i can't escape myself.
i'm trapped in my body and it's like i don't know how to operate it,
why doesn't this thing come with some sort of a manual?
i've never had this many good days in a row.
i've never had this many good days after being stuck with myself for hours on end.
it's crazy.
i can't wrap my head around it and i don't know what i've done to deserve this?
maybe someone up there felt bad for everything that happened to me last year?
that's the only thing that comes close to making sense in my head.
i do know that i'll never take a good day for granted ever again because i don't know if they're numbered or not.

i've had so many bad days and my luck isn't any better than that so i know it has to be a matter of time before this hits the fan and i'm stuck crying on the floor again.
i'm slowly feeling more like a person though which has to be a good thing right?
to no longer feel like a machine and to feel like a human?
i'd like to think so.
i know i've always been a person though because of all the emotions i feel,
but i never truly felt like i was living and moments just seemed fleeting.
i'm spiraling and there's nothing to grab onto to keep me upright.
i'm falling and i have nobody to catch me.
fell off the tightrope and now it's just choking me.
it's been a while since i've been encompassed by this feeling and i've almost missed it.
almost.
that's the keyword here.
might have missed it slightly but never fully.
this feeling of restlessness has to be one of my least favorite things to experience.
i lie here in my bed pulling at my hair and frantically looking around the room for something.
i never know what it is that i'm looking for,
i just know that once i find it,
it seems almost impossible that it could've been anything else.

i think most of the time i might be looking for subtle reminders of you.
anytime i look at the middle of the carpet where the television now sits,
i see you sitting there that night in september, in your blue hoodie and your work pants.
you've got smokey in your arms and you look so at peace.
i look over there often.
you always had a demeanor about you that never failed to calm me down.
i guess that's what love is right?
you see them and suddenly it's as if all your problems just fade into the background and it's just them.
i miss the wave of calm that you brought to me.
i hope that you see me sitting on your couch sometimes or in your passenger seat and i hope it causes your chest to ache too.
why am i writing about you again?!
i literally wrote today about how everything i write always ends up having you in it.
GET OUT OF MY HEAD!
let me exist without you.

words.

"sadness", what a funny word for an emotion so great.
an emotion full of hurt,
and loss,
and mourning,
and pain.
sadness is the word used when you talk about missing someone,
after missing the sun after a long week of rain,
after mourning the loss of love,
after thinking about the "once was" or the "might have been"
emotions are such a significant part of us and all we can do is name them.
we name them with such insignificant letters in hopes of justifying the feelings they bring us.
no matter what we call it, no word will ever be able to perfectly encompass that emptiness that sadness brings us.

1:54 am.

it's one fifty-four in the morning and all i can do is write about you.
what the hell is that about?
i still miss you.
i still haven't reached that place where i can think of you and feel nothing.
i hope you're doing well.
i hope you think of me.
please think of me.
i hope it was hard for you—leaving me.
why should i have to suffer if you're not?
it's not fair that i have to be stuck here crying when you probably never shed a tear.
i hope it hits you all at once,
what you lost.
i'll get better one day.
i know i will.
i can't wait for then.
when i'll be able to see you and not hurt.
i can't wait for one fifty-four in the morning and i'm okay.

cycles.

it seems there's a constant cycle of usage in my life.
i've never realized it before but i think i've finally figured it out?
we've gone from talking every day, to not talking at all, and you say it's because you're busy with work and school is starting back up soon and i get that, really i do.
yet somehow we went from texting 24/7, to snapchatting and texting, to snapchatting, to just chatting, and then it became one dark snap a day to keep that stupid streak alive.
the streak ended, much like our conversations that i used to stay awake for every night just so i could talk to you.
you used me for my body even though you've got a girl of your own, you found it necessary to single me out.
when i finally gave in and gave you what you wanted, you stopped talking to me.
you pinky promised that i'd never lose you.
but i'm watching it happen and there's absolutely nothing that i can do about it and i feel like screaming and crying and fighting until you realize that i am still here on the sidelines.
i'm on the fucking sidelines and you're just showing me that i never had a chance on the playing field anyways.

be okay.

i made the decision to remove myself from your life.
after all that's what you wanted right?
you wanted me gone.
you ignore me for so long although you act like nothing's wrong but your words or lack thereof says something completely different.
why won't you just be honest with me?
i refuse to be used by you anymore for your needs when you give me nothing in return.
i refuse to be just another girl in your life as you push me to the side for someone better than me.
you can't make me feel like less than i'm worth ever again.
it took me so long to come to this conclusion.
i waited two months after the messages stopped coming in,
i tried so hard to give you the benefit of the doubt time and time again and i made up so many excuses in my head for you.
i shouldn't have to justify your actions to me.
i shouldn't have to convince myself that we're friends.
i shouldn't have to feel like this.
yet i do time and time again because you're all i have.
without you, i don't know who i am.
i'm nervous about how you'll react to this.
i left your number unblocked just in case you need to say something or if you ever need me.
i don't think you ever will and that kills me.
i need you.

so much.
and no matter how you act now,
i know that at some point you felt the same exact way.
what happened?
what happened to us?
i think about that all the time.
i don't think i'll ever be able to wrap my head around it.
if you're just going through something and pushing away the people you're closest to and you need me after all this is done...
i don't think i'd ever be able to forgive myself for leaving you.
god, i hope you're okay,
i hope that's not the case.
the thought of you not being okay makes me sick to my stomach.
i only want the best for you and i'm sorry that i couldn't be that for you.
please be okay,
for both of us.

replacement.

time and time again you show me who you really are.
underneath the façade of the stone-cold, hard-ass, we both know how much of a kind-hearted teddy bear you can really be.
although as of late, underneath you've been so dark and terrifying.
you constantly keep pushing me away and you act as if i don't exist.
any other time we're attached at the hip.
what's going on?
won't you please let me in?
all i want is to bring you back.
where did you go?
regardless of how many times you push me away, i'll always run back to you.
you're my rock and i'm yours.
you can try to deny that as much as you want but it's quite obvious to our friends and myself that that's the case.
who's this new person that you're always messaging and laughing with?
you can't see me because you'd rather spend time with them?
my calls and messages because i'm worried about you, go unanswered because you've spent the day with them.
i guess it was only a matter of time before you replaced me with someone else.

i hope they figure you out quickly, or soon, they'll be on the chopping block too.

i don't need you.

sometimes i worry about what might happen if you ever read any of these or at least the ones about you.
would you even be able to tell which ones are about you?
would you even care?
i write about you all the time and you consume my every thought and i can't seem to get your stupid face out of my head and i think of it often.
you're still one of the most beautiful things i've had the joy of looking at.
there's nothing more i want than for you to go away.
sadly the image of you is burned in my mind.
i wish maybe you would read these.
maybe then you'd be able to process what you put me through and just how i felt for you.
we both know that when you love,
you love h a r d.
but what you don't know is that i'm exactly the same way.
the way i felt about you rivals how you felt about her.
you didn't know that because i never told you.
i didn't tell you so many things that i should've and i'll regret that for the rest of my life.
maybe it's good that we never worked out because how fiercely we love could've torn the world apart.
the fire that would result from our love colliding could've shattered time and space.
we were a force to be reckoned with.

you and i were unstoppable and that's why we never worked because we simply would've been too powerful and nothing that good can last.
"nothing gold can stay."
i think about that line often in reference to you.
you were my golden thing and you couldn't have ever lasted in my love.
my love transcends the known universe,
there is so much that i know and so much left for me to learn and you wouldn't have been able to last long here.
i'm fine with that because i have myself at the end of the day and i'm getting used to her.
she's fun to be around.
i make myself laugh so often it's almost as if i'm not alone.
i don't need you or your love.
and i never did.
it's taken me so long to realize that.

second choice.

seems like no matter how hard i try or how much i change myself,
i always seem to be second choice to literally any other person.
i really let myself believe it was different this time.
how naïve of me.
i've started to rethink a lot of things these past few months.
when did that start?
i guess i can say i pinpointed that change in behavior.
i don't think you're even aware of it happening.
maybe that's for the best.
obviously i'm no good.
i guess i'm damaged goods.
second choice is nothing new for me.
doesn't mean it hurts any less than the last time.
you're the last thing i need right now on top of all the other things happening in my life.
i'm sorry i'm not good enough for you.
or for anyone.
i'll try harder.
although maybe i should give it up.
i'm tired of this.
everything hurts.
my heart is heavy.
second choice is my place.

miss you.

it's still so weird not having you in my life.
sometimes i miss you so much i can hardly breathe.
days like today i struggle the most without you.
all i want is to talk to you...
i miss the small conversations.
i miss calling you at two in the morning just to hear your voice.
i remember one time i missed you so much i called you at two in the morning and you answered and told me you were showering.
for some reason, you kept me on the line and kept talking to me.
you stayed on the phone with me for the next two hours while we talked about anything and everything, as we so often did.
it's one of my favorite memories.
there was always something to talk about, no matter what time of day it was.
it's such a simple thing, talking on the phone.
i can't believe i took it for granted.
there's nothing more i'd want right now than to call you up and catch up.
seeing how we're no longer in each other's lives, i think it'd be best if i didn't call.
your laugh and your voice were easily one of my favorite sounds in the world.
i'm glad i have so many videos of it.

i have one video, you were playing fortnite, as always.
you had just gotten first place in duos, how wild is that?
i zoomed in on the screen, then panned to you and you had that goofy smirk on your face, and you're looking at me and say "it was all me i killed all of them." and you looked so proud of yourself.
i remember watching you play that stupid game for hours on end just so i could spend time with you.
every minute i spent with you was a great one.
even the ones we fought in.
i even kind of miss fighting with you.
maybe one day i'll reach out.

cast out to sea.

the nightmares are back, yet again.
the villain is different this time.
instead of seeing he who shall not be named,
it's you.
the other night i dreamt that i was cast out to sea during a typhoon.
i knew it was you who'd left me to die at sea.
i think that's the best metaphor i could've asked for.
everything in my life had hit the fan at once.
i'd never been lower in my life and yet in the midst of all of it you decided that was the best time for you to bow out of my life.
you left me to die in the middle of the ocean,
you left me to fend for myself after everything we'd been through.
i talked you down from so many cliffs that you were standing on, i helped you through hell and brought you back, but when i'm asking for the same thing i get abandoned?
i never imagined that you out of all the people in my life would be the one to leave me.
i got pulled under by the current and i was screaming for you, why can't you hear me?
the water filled my lungs and everything was turning black.
i never thought i'd see the sun again.
then i woke up and realized i wasn't drowning.
i feel free now.

i learned to live without you. i still miss you but i know i don't need you.
i'm a tough swimmer now.

before and after.

i'm sitting hopelessly on my floor,
pulling at my hair and running my hands across my face in a desperate attempt to feel something.
i feel so unbelievably lost,
if that's even the right way to explain this.
i feel like a meteor crashed into me and i'm stuck picking up the pieces and i have to put them together and figure out who the hell i am.
i do this so often and somehow i keep getting it wrong.
the pieces get put back in the wrong order.
i need to figure it out.
figure that out and everything will be okay again right?
maybe he'll come back.
no i don't need him.
i'm fine by myself.
i always used to think "i was fine before him and i'll be fine without him" but here i am.
without him.
and i'm not fine.
i don't even know what fine is anymore.
it's just "before and after".
i'm stuck in the after and it's nothing like the book.
maybe it is.
there's emotional and mental abuse in the book and that's really all i ever got from him anyways.

however tessa still gets her happily ever after with harry and i'm stuck here...on my floor.
i mean did i really do anything different before him?
i can't even remember who i was.
i can't picture my life before him.
he came into my world and rocked it on its axis.
nothing will ever be the same and i've accepted that because what's the point in denying it?
before him was dull and the days seemed to blur together.
during him was bright and electric.
after him is just bleak and hopeless.

i think i still love you.

everyone always underestimated how much i cared about you, although everyone knew to some degree that i had feelings for you.
i loved you.
loving you was as easy as breathing,
i didn't have to think about it.
i loved you with every atom in my body.
and then you left, and i was still in love with you.
then i was in love with something that no longer existed in my life and i still did it as simply as breathing.
someone came into work today wearing the same cologne as you and i had to step off the floor and go to the back.
it brought back too many painful memories.
i almost started crying right then and there.
isn't that silly?
i know if someone came around wearing my perfume you wouldn't bat an eye.
it's been a year so why do i still feel this way?
is it because i never got closure?
why do i still care?
i hate that i still feel this way.
why do you do this to me?
you still consume almost every one of my thoughts and i know you don't spare me a single one.
i'm not who i once was because i gave you every single aspect of myself and now i have to reinvent myself.

and do you know what the worst part of it all is?
i think i still love you.

dream a little dream of me too.

i think a part of me will always love you,
i've tried to deny it for so long because of how you treated me.
you always treated me like i was less of a human and i let you—because i was so smitten with you.
not with you, more so the idea of you.
i was in love with the idea of you.
i don't think i'll ever be able to accept that i don't love you anymore.
sometimes i think i've come around to the idea that i don't love you and i don't care anymore,
and i'm almost immediately proven wrong.
you appear in my dreams almost constantly and just like clockwork, you were there last night.
i'm not sure why my mind likes to torture me like this.
you were there and so were all of our old friends except this time we seemed to be dating and everything was great.
that's how i knew it was a dream because of how well everything was going.
i was sitting on your lap with your arms in the dream and you were whispering some joke into my ear and laughing.
that's something that rarely ever happens for real and it only happened when we were in the comfort of your car or on your couch.
you weren't very much into pda when it came to me anyways, everything between us happened in privacy.

i know deep down that i shouldn't feel this way and i know it's wrong of me to still think of you like this,
god i hope you think of me.
i hope that you're scared to lose the memory of me too.
i hope that you remember me every time you get into the car,
i hope you see my shadow in the passenger seat of your car.
i hope you see me sitting on your piano bench every time you turn your computer on,
and i hope you see me on your couch when you watch television.
i hope your fingers itch to message me.
i hope the memory of me haunts you forever as you're haunting me.
spare me a thought every now and again.
dream a little dream of me.

mistakes.

i've made some mistakes in my life, that part is so obviously clear.
maybe getting involved with you was one of them, but knowing what i know now and feeling the way i do, i know i wouldn't trade those days for anything else.
no matter what i always find myself coming back to you and find you running across my mind, even when i know you shouldn't.
i spend most of my days crippled by anxiety and the constant stress turning in my stomach leaving my unable to eat or think.
i've barely ate more than once a day in months, and i don't think mom and dad have caught on yet.
you plague every thought i have and you invade every dream.
i find myself messaging you, always starting with "hi i'm probably annoying you and i'm sorry for that but", and always ending with the same result...nothing.
not a sound.
not even a glance in the hallways in the school we've been attending for years.
it's like i no longer exist in your perfect little world and maybe that's for the best?
maybe i'll realize that i don't need you either and maybe i'll start eating again soon and maybe my stress and anxiety won't be as crippling.
maybe one day i won't think about you every second of every day and you won't take up every dream i have.

one day you'll be nothing more than a speck of dust i forgot to clean off the shelf and that day can't come soon enough.

365 days ago.

three hundred and sixty-five days ago i was with my two best friends on the planet.
we went to chilis and back to one of their houses.
he played fortnite and i stood behind him playing with his hair, and olivia sat on the piano bench looking at memes and watching us.
i wore his burgundy sweater because i was cold and also it smelled like him so why not.
i remember i stopped playing with his hair because my arms got tired and he threw a tiny fit because of it.
i put my hands back in his hair to help ease his frustration at the game.
at some point we all ended up on the couch, cuddled together, watching who knows what it was.
my head on his chest and his fingers in my hair, his head on liv's chest and we're all laughing and having a great time.
i remember thinking that i'd love to live in that moment for the rest of my life.
sadly, moments don't last forever and happiness is fleeting.
a month later he would tell me that my time was up and he would step out of my life.
i'd be left in the dark with a bleeding heart.
three hundred and sixty-five days later and i still think of him.
i remember every detail about him.
from the way his eyes lit up to the way his lip curled up when he smiled that stupid smile i loved so much.

i think i'll always remember him, he was my first real love. hopefully three hundred and sixty-five days from now this ache will be gone.

fragile.

everything is so fragile.
you and i, whether we're aware of it or not, or even realize the extent of it,
we're as fragile as a sheet of glass.
one wrong move or touch and we'll shatter into a million different pieces that can't be placed back together with a simple,
"i'm sorry".
sometimes those pieces can be glued back together if someone says the right thing, and even then it's only a matter of time before we break again.
they'll never fit back together quite right, there's always going to be a stray fragment left or an edge that's a little too rough that results in someone getting hurt.
it'll be a bit different and it'll take a while to adapt to that change of not being completely right, but you'll get there one day.
i think by now at least all my pieces are a little rough around the edges.
i've even gotten hurt myself trying to pick all my pieces back up, and i've thought "how messed up is that? i'm trying to help myself yet i got cut? what sense does that make?"
i've always had that comparison in my head to glass and fragility, and how i seem to always break after one wrong move.

the past few years it seems as if all i've done is break and i haven't had time to fix myself so by now my glass shards have been reduced to sand.
i might give up.
nothing i do or say will fix this.
i'm nothing but a bunch of shards asking for help.
can someone help this pile of shards?
i didn't think so.

wrong impression.

i don't understand how this keeps happening to me?
i was talking to a curly black-haired boy with piercing blue eyes,
we were talking for months and you seemed like you were really interested in me too.
you drove almost two hours to see me on new years,
so forgive me if i got the wrong impression from that.
and you keep talking about how you miss me and you want to see me but none of your actions or other words suggests that.
we made it through six of the harry potter movies and now we'll never finish them because you left.
when we spent the night together
which was one of the scariest things i've ever done considering everything that's happened to me,
it still is undeniably one of my favorite memories.
we had so much fun,
from trying to watch "a quiet place", with you saying "why is the movie so quiet",
to us failing to watch it because i decided to take a nap.
that was hard for me because of what's happened to me.
the fact that i was able to sleep around you says so much but i don't think it even phased you.
then me waking up and us going back to the bedroom to both nap and us waking up and it leading to skin on skin under the sheets.

i even had fun when you drove us to taco bell and then decided you wanted cookout and proceeded to drive us to two different ones because we messed up the drive-thru line at the first one.
singing hannah montana in the car with you will always be something i'll hold close to my heart.
we went home and ate while we watched some of glamngore's videos and you didn't complain that she was doing makeup you were just happy to be spending time with me.
we went to bed and in the morning we woke up and yet again couldn't keep our hands off each other.
we got breakfast at ihop and went to the movies on a proper date and spent the rest of the afternoon walking around the mall and you showed me where you're from.
so please forgive me if i got the wrong impression.
i seem to always get it wrong.
how could i have gotten it wrong this time?
everything was matched with the same damn energy and he seemed to care about me and he didn't use me for my body and he liked the way i look.
so why the hell has this happened to me again?
why do i feel like it was a breakup when we were never actually together?
why do i continue to waste months of my life on guys who only want me for a minuscule moment of the day?
do i have a sign on my back that says "please lead me on and then leave"?
i just don't get it.

and his instagram comments and anonymous posts are all girls telling him how attractive he is and how much they want him and they ask him if he's talking to anyone and he always says no.
so what am i to him?
nothing?
dirt under his feet?
why does this hurt so damn much?
this is ridiculous.
you ignore me most of the day now and i know you're not busy because you don't go to school and you don't have a job yet you can't pick up the phone and send me a quick text during the day?
it's gotten to the point where i can't recall our last conversation.
it's not as if i miss you.
i honestly don't.
i just want to know how i let this happen again.
i'm tired of temporary people.
i can't believe i got the wrong impression again.

karma is one hell of a bitch.

i thought about you today.
i sat there and i thought about if you'd ever try to come back after you've grown up and you try to apologize for the way you treated me,
i wouldn't ever be able to forgive you.
it's not like this was middle school when you played your stupid games.
you were a high school graduate and you had nothing to gain from doing it.
you did it out of immaturity and malice.
you knew what you were doing and that was so painfully clear as you laughed with our friend about what you were doing.
there's never going to be an excuse for the way you treated me so you can try every single one the book has,
it won't change the way i feel about you.
i will always loathe you no matter what you try to do to fix it.
you did it twice!
there's no excusing that horrific behavior when it was repeated.
i don't think i'll ever be able to fully wrap my head around it.
i do know the way i feel about you is strong enough to move mountains with.
you should watch your back.
you don't know what i'm capable of.
i hope that nobody ever loves you.
i hope that you never know the joy that is love.
i hope someone plays games with you as you did to me.

i hope someone calls you an object.
i hope you open up to someone and they laugh about it with their friends.
i hope everything you did to me comes back to you tenfold.
and who knows it just might.

the universe has grown dark.

i used to look at you like you'd hung the moon in the sky.
you were the center of my universe.
everything in my life revolved around you, i guess in a way i put my life on hold for you.
i was always trying to hold your attention for as long as you'd grace me with it.
i've never looked at anyone else like that or let alone have everything i do be about someone else.
you were all i wanted.
the world around us could be crumbling down but i wouldn't have batted an eye as long as i had you by my side.
it's been a little over a year now without the moon and the sky is so dark.
has it always been so empty and void?
i haven't seen the stars in a while either.
you left and took it all with you, you stole my moon and my stars.
you went off into the unknown and you took it all with you.
how could you do that to me? i thought i meant something to you...
sometimes i hope you're suffering just as much as i have been.
that you've been dealing with the same amount of hurt, if not more, because of the way you treated me.
you always treated me like i was less than you as if i wasn't important enough to be in your life.

then i come to my senses and realize that i'd never want that for you.
somehow even after all of this, i could never wish this kind of hurt on you.
i could never wish any kind of pain on you.
a year and a half without you, and you still mean too much to me for me to ever hate you.
i want to hate you so bad.
i owe it to myself to hate you.
you deserve for me to hate you—yet i can't bring myself to.
i still think about you like you hang the moon in the sky.
i look at our old memories and smile fondly remembering the days when the moonlight was blinding.
it's been a year and a half without you and i still miss you like the day you left.

space.

maybe the stars never aligned for you and i.
i think that was our problem.
it's no secret that i believe the stars hold secrets about us and our futures.
the universe was sending us a message and we were too blind to see until it was too late.
from the beginning, things never seemed to work for us, everything was always push and shove.
i think you and i were just simply never meant to be.
you must understand, my love, when i say "we need space",
i'm saying "i think we must look at the stars and see how they're not looking back".
we're simply two star crossed lovers who were never meant to beat the test of time.
we were doomed from the start.
did we just meet at the wrong time or was it something more than that?
can you even remember when we met?
i bet you can remember when it all fell apart and simply didn't click anymore.
nobody ever remembers the start of things,
they only remember the messy end.

trying my best.

i've spent so long trying:
to understand,
to make peace,
to breathe,
to sleep,
to eat,
to calm down,
to find myself.
i've never stopped trying, despite how it looks and what you might think.
i don't think i'll ever understand why.
and it's far too soon to try and make any sort of peace with it.
i have enormous weights on my chest.
i see you in every single one of my dreams and when i close my eyes.
i have absolutely no appetite.
i'm lost in the abyss of my own mind.
you ruined me.
you stole who i was in jacksonville and i'm never going to get her back.
you absolutely destroyed everything that i was.
i shouldn't have to live like this.
yet here i am.
you're everywhere!
i can't escape.
i'm trapped in my mind.

i've done everything i can to get out.
i don't think you even realize the extent of what you did to me.
i could write about it all day and you'd never be able to understand unless you had it happen to you.
i'm never getting over this.

peace at last?

it's always odd watching things unfold and not being able to change anything.
sadly this isn't chess, and i can't just pick us up and move us accordingly.
i feel like i'm floating above my body watching everything happen.
it's been that way for a while, i can't even remember the last time i truly felt like myself.
as of late i've been thinking about you more—but not in the way you're hoping.
i've been trying to give myself that sense of closure that you never gave me.
i'm so desperate for it that i dreamt it up last night, isn't that sad?
i woke up with a newly found sense of peace, or i thought i did.
if i'm so at peace, why do tears keep welling up in my eyes?
if i'm so at peace, why does my chest feel like it has dumbbells on it?
if i'm so at peace, why does the room look like it's spinning?
why does this keep happening to me?
you've been gone for over a year now, it's been well over three hundred and sixty-five days, so why can't you just leave me alone?
you still plague every corner of my mind, you're in the most accessed parts, and you're hidden back in the shadows.

whenever something happens, you're still, unfortunately, the first person i want to tell.
when i see something funny, i still want to send it to you first.
it's not fair how i'm left aching for you when you probably don't feel the same.
it's so gut-wrenching to think about that,
—you not missing me.
i gave you all of me and i thought i had all of you.
i never saw it coming.
these changes happen so gradually that one day i woke up and you simply weren't here.
you phased me out of your life day by day and i was too blind to see it.
you always told me, "i always expect to see you by my side", those words haunt me at night you know?
it's been over a year of not being by your side but i still feel your presence with everything i do.
i can't even remember who i was before you.
that's the scariest part in my opinion.
do you miss me?
do you dream of me too?
do you even spare me a thought?
i wish i could go back in time and change everything.

hurting.

heavy heart,
heavy eyes,
hurting heart,
hurting eyes.

hurt, according to webster's dictionary, is:
causing physical pain or injury, suffer pain, cause mental pain or distress.

and lately that's all i've known.
the weight of the world seems to sit on my shoulders.
day after day after day i wake up and do the same thing i did the day before, nothing ever seems to change!

oh how my head and heart ache for something to free them from this pain.
i've never known to hurt like this, it's all uncharted territory for me.

broken, that's how i feel, used goods.
one of these days i'm going to crack and i don't know if i have it in me to put myself back together.

trust issues.

it's been a year since we last spoke and i still haven't been able to figure out why you did what you did.
my cheeks still burn hot with embarrassment.
my chest still flares up with anger.
my fists still clench with rage.
i hope one day i'll be able to move past this.
i think i'm angrier at myself because this wasn't the first time you did this to me.
it was the second.
how did i let it happen again?
i thought you'd changed.
it really seemed like you had.
i think of it sometimes and it still makes my head spin.
it's definitely ruined me.
i second guess everything anyone says to me because i can't believe that anyone would be nice to me without ill intentions.
they're just building me up so they can tear me apart as you did.
i'm afraid i'm nothing but a joke to them.
you read about these kinds of games in books and you see them happen in movies but you never think they're real.
you never think someone is cruel enough to do it in real life.
i can't believe that someone that knows the same people i know could act this way.
was that the end goal?
to mess me up so completely that i become a paranoid mess?

i can't take anyone for who they are because i'm scared they'll hurt me like you have.
i can't believe in the few months we knew each other you caused me years of issues.

burn up.

you always used to tell me that you'd burn up everything i had and that you'd leave me broken.
i always used to deny it because i simply couldn't, or rather i wouldn't dare imagine my life without you in it.
we'd instantly clicked from the moment we met and our friendship only got messier from there.
the line between friend and lover blurred too many times that it made my head spin.
i think that's why everything crumbled the way it did.
we'd depended on each other too much, well at least i depended on you too much.
between the late night conversations and the one too many touches and kisses,
somehow things got twisted in my head and i seemed to make myself believe that, at least for a little while, you'd felt the same way i did.
i'd make an excuse for everything you did simply because i was falling in love with you.
it was like loving a brick wall, it was cold and at times it really hurt.
i never seemed to know where we stood.
eventually, i seemed to have stopped making up excuses for you and i realized how one-sided everything was.
i would give and you would take, and take and take until there was nothing left for me to give.
i seemed to have lost myself within you.

you broke me.
as much as i hate to admit it, you were right.
you burned me up and left me a shell.

a ramble from 2016.

longing is an odd feeling. it's even odder when you don't know what it is you're longing for.
i long for so many things but most of the time it's for another feeling such as happiness or the feeling of being complete.
i long to be somewhere new but somewhere old at the same time.
new to me but old to the world around it.
it's these places that i often find myself.
to be in a place that is torn apart from the elements and abuse from rowdy teenagers who often spend nights destroying whatever they touch.
you never notice the wonders around you until you can see what it becomes when you're gone.
hold on to what you have because tomorrow is never promised.
betrayal is an odd feeling as well.
it's odd to be betrayed over and over again especially when it's by the same person.
most people would have given up and i guess that's the biggest difference between you and i.
you'd never take anyone's crap whereas i'm constantly being stepped on.
you're desensitized and you don't care about hurting someone whereas the first thought on my mind is how something will affect someone's feelings.
i care too much and you care too little.

we've been friends for a while now and i don't think you know me at all.
i knew so much about you i could tell you a lot more about yourself than you could ever tell me.
i could make a list of things i liked about you.
i could've been the greatest friend you'd ever have but you had to throw all of that away.
for a stupid joke.
you had so many chances and you just threw them all away.
you blew them away like leaves on a summer breeze.
i would've gone to the ends of the earth for you.
you'd always expected there to be another chance as if this was some sort of wishing well.
i've seen what you do and i've seen the destruction that you've caused.
i've seen the rubble and the disaster that you leave behind.
i've lived in it.
i'm living in it.
you ruined the girl i thought i was.
i don't know who i am and you don't care.
you never cared.
you call me names and you move on with your happy little life.
i've come to terms with everything you've said and done.
i'm not okay with it and i don't know if i ever will be.
you've done wrong by me too many times and i'm through playing your pathetic little games.
i regret ever knowing you.

i regret letting you into my life.
i regret meeting you.
i want my life back.
fuck you.

for ** part I.

i told you once,
in one of our many phone calls that took place over the span of the month we were "friends",
"i believe there's some sort of good somewhere in you."
despite all your flaws and the way you had treated me prior to that point in time,
i truly believed you had changed.
you made it believable.
they say drunk words are sober thoughts so who was i to deny that when you were crying drunk on the phone upset that you had hurt me.
knowing what i know now, at this point in time,
and feeling the way that you made me feel.
i wholeheartedly take that back.
i truly don't believe that anywhere in your heart and soul that there is anything good there.
your heart is pure obsidian and you find joy out of hurting other people.
it's a wonder to me how you have any friends at all.
we have a few mutual friends and one of them, you told them everything, and she decided it wasn't worth telling me.
i guess that should've said something then.
i hope you never know what it's like to be truly happy.
i hope nobody ever truly loves you, someone like you doesn't deserve that.
i hope someone makes you feel the way you made me feel.

for ** part II.

people aren't objects for you to use at your disposal.
people have feelings and your relentless torment can make such a mess of things and tear them apart.
you wore me down with your kind words and your games, though i suppose the kind words were just part of that game.
you play these sick twisted games and you get such a kick out of it, you think they're hilarious.
you tell our friend what i've said and then ask her how you should reply to it.
you ask our friend how i feel about you because that just fuels the game on even farther.
you're toxic and you're twisted it's a wonder to me how you have any friends at all.
i think about your drunk words all the time.
how many of them were lies?
did you mean any of it?
when did this stupid game start?
why me?
for me, you sharing everything we did to our friend and our coworkers was the worst thing you could have done to me.
maybe if i got you drunk enough and asked you the million questions i have floating around in my head i'd get some answers.
or maybe you'd just lie to me again.
all you know how to do is lie.

i wouldn't be able, to tell the truth between the truth and a lie, when it came to you.
you seemed like you actually cared about me, and i'm so stupid for believing that.
you only cared to tell people what happened.
you told me my opinion mattered.
it only mattered so you could see just how deep your claws were in my back.
you fueled my insecurities and somehow gave me more than i started with.
how did you manage to do that?
i'm never going to be able to trust anyone ever again.
what the hell is your problem?
i never did anything to you other than try to be your friend.
was that so wrong?
i've never met someone like you, pure evil.
you're worse than any villain in any movie.

i was #1.

i've always had an issue with thinking i mean more to people than i really do.
it's only gotten worse after i was told i'm one of the only people you tell everything to.
now i see that i'm only important when you need something.
i assumed you'd always need me regardless of what was happening.
you'd always need me by your side.
i realize that i've been replaced.
i'm used to being your number one.
i know for at least a little while i was.
now i'm a nobody.
i don't have anyone that needed me the way you did and i feel so utterly useless.
you told me that you'd always need me so why am i watching everything from the outside?
trying to think about how much you mean to someone will really mess you up.
especially when you use it as some sort of measurement for your own self-worth.
thinking in general usually does that for me.
i was your rock and now you have a new one and i don't know what to do with myself.
i hate that it's come to this.
i just want to be needed by you.

regrets.

i have many regrets.
some of them are things that i've never been able to control so how is it that i'm able to regret them?
i've spent a lot of time pondering over them and i still don't know what one i'd consider being my biggest.
the list is incredibly long and would take too long to explain or share with you.
i've been trying to entertain the idea of adding you to that list but i don't think you'd ever make the final cut.
if i do add you to it you never last very long before i scratch your name out,
you've been redacted a lot actually.
you changed me for the better.
yes i gained some trust issues and now i have an even worse abandonment problem...
but i swear i've changed and i've grown.
i've learned so much from you.
regardless of those lessons i know i learned something.
every moment i got to spend with you was a precious gift that i'll never be able to get rid of.
i thank you for that.
i found a sense of "home" within you.
and i'd like to think you found home within me.
my list of regrets is mostly the things i didn't say to you or the things i never did with you.
granted i did think we had more time.

i didn't think it would end so abruptly.
as i sit here and think some more on this,
i've decided that my biggest regret is walking away from you.

winter thoughts.

the familiar chill of charlotte winters seeps into my bones draining me of all warmth.
i begin to ponder upon the last year of my life as i so often do this late at night.
according to my snapchat memories, a year ago today i was with a dear friend at their house.
at their house were some of the finest people i'd ever had the pleasure of meeting.
well i thought they were but as time went on i realized that they weren't as great as i thought.
i'm not sure when i realized that or how i finally did,
it's odd to think about that.
i pondered on that for one hundred and eighty-two days.
i never got my answer.
i came to terms with it,
or so i thought.
i started rethinking it when he wished me happy birthday...
why?
why would he do that?
we ended on such horrible terms.
plus he always treated me like garbage.
i spent another two weeks thinking about that.
i can't believe i spent so much time thinking about someone who i know wouldn't spend more than one second on me.
the cold air in my bones seems to always remind me of you.
and your colder than ice heart.

back to the start.

i was re-reading my older works tonight and i noticed that a few could be about a few different people.
how fun!
that just means i was dumb enough to put myself back it the same situation with multiple people and learn nothing from past mistakes.
i like to think that as of right now, 2020, i'm much smarter than my previous 2017 self.
i hope so at least.
i just don't understand how i can keep hurting my own feelings.
it's my own fault i ended up back in these situations and i still don't know how that even happened!
i hope i'll be smarter down the road and at least recognize what is happening.

update: i wasn't any smarter down the road.

a ramble about hurt and hurricane florence.

i tried to take all of your hurt and make it my own.
i tried to free you from the thoughts in your head that tore you up late at night.
i tried to take your demons and put them on me to free you.
i tried to take every ounce of negative energy out of your life and deal with it for you.
i tried to put every burden of yours onto my shoulders to ease the weight on yours.
you had demons that you didn't deserve and i tried so damn hard to get rid of them for you.
i didn't realize that in the process i was losing myself.
i became a shell of a person filled with things that bothered you and it was smothering me.
it was like i didn't know how to exist if you weren't relying on me to help you.
i truly felt like i couldn't function without you.
i think you noticed that much.
that i lost myself,
or that i wasn't really me anymore.
you were always great at picking up on things like that and i've never been able to understand it.
you didn't try to help me through it.
or maybe you thought you were helping when you left me.
you walked away like i was nobody to you,
like the numerous late-night calls had never happened,

you acted as if i was just a stranger you had bumped into and you kept walking.
i wish it was harder for you to leave me.
i wish you found yourself getting attached to people.
i wish it had hurt you to leave me.
we were friends for a little over two years and we had been to hell and back during that time,
and yet leaving had never seemed so easy.
i'm still here trying to make sense of it.
i'm spiraling.
i can't even listen to the artists that we both love.
it took me a year and a half to be able to listen to eden again, and every time i hear something from the pray for the wicked album i can't help but think of you and i at that concert.
you live in every corner of my mind and i long for the day where i won't think of you.
when you first left me it was nearly impossible to function.
and every time i saw something funny my fingers itched to send it to you,
that urge has left me thankfully, though unwillingly, i have no way of getting in contact with you.
not that i'd really want to anymore.
at first, i did, for sure, to ask you where it all went wrong.
now i know that this was inevitable and there was nothing that i could have done to save us no matter how hard i tried.
i was always trying to save you from every negative thing that would ever come your way and for a really long time, i was successful.

you can't even deny that.
things didn't really ever get truly ugly in your life until her and hurricane florence.
i don't know what happened that week.
we went to the room as friends and everything after that felt off.
everyone in our group left that room a different person.
it's always me making sure everyone is okay and doing well.
nobody ever really checks up on me,
especially that week.
i was running on pure adrenaline trying to make sure that everyone was okay and not hurting themselves.
between you and her and our other friends who all seemed to have a crisis going on at the same time and putting everything on me,
i didn't have any energy left.
i was drowning in everyone's issues and i didn't have time to save myself.
the worst part is that not a single person noticed.
i took so many breaks sitting on the staircases outside of our apartment because i felt like i couldn't breathe.
i walked the building so many times just in an attempt to get away from it all.
now that week is long gone but i can still feel myself there.
i left part of myself in apartment a215.

right place, wrong time.

there's been a few people in my life that have made me think of "right place, wrong time".
i think the only thing that ever stopped him and i was he had too much on his plate,
we connected on every single level and talking always came easy to us.
it's odd how easy it was.
if things just happened to be a little further down in our timeline we could've been great and i think he knows it too.
he tells me that he misses me and that he thinks of me often and those words make my heart soar.
it makes me sad to know that he probably has other people he talks to so i try my best to convince myself that isn't the case and he's different but when you live so far away you can only tell yourself that for so long before you stop believing it.
i know deep down in my soul at some point it would've worked for us.
i'll hold out hope that one day i'll see you in the right place at the right time.

wilmington.

standing there with my feet in the sand in wilmington after running away from my problems.
the biting cold wind whipping my hair in every direction blinding me.
i can't help but wonder how i got here.
when did i become someone who ran from her issues?
when did i become someone who couldn't face the voices in her head?
when did i let my problems dictate my actions?
when did i become so incredibly broken that i couldn't fix it?
when did i begin thinking that running away was an option?
everything in my life seemed to be moving so fast.
everything still is moving too fast.
i feel like i'm being tossed around in the wind.
it feels like i haven't moved in a month but the world around me is.
have i moved?
everything is different now but it's also still painfully the same.
how does that happen?
i know it's been about six months so it's illogical to think that i haven't moved but maybe it was just illogical of me to think that things would change.
i've lost so many people and while i have gained some, it's nothing compared to those not with me anymore.
i ran away to the beach to escape all of it and try to make sense of everything so why do i feel so confused?

why can i not seem to make sense of anything?
this isn't fair.
why can i still feel the wind in my hair and the sand under my feet?
how can i still smell the sea breeze and feel the sun on my face?
am i still on that beach in wilmington?

four years and twenty-four hours.

it's strange to think about how much changed in twenty-four hours.
somehow we went from texting constantly and planning to facetime later that same night to you not returning my messages and removing me on all social media.
then i come to find out that it all adds up because you're suddenly at your ex-girlfriend's house despite you telling me that your parents won't let you out of the house due to the virus.
i just need to know is it something that i did or something that i said?
we have a lot of mutual friends and they all say the same thing that this is just how you are and i shouldn't take it too personally but it's almost always my fault.
it doesn't help when you've told me how much you missed me and that there were times you wanted to reach out to me when we lost touch.
you even told me that you didn't want to ghost me so what the hell happened?
what changed in the length of a day?
it's been keeping me awake trying to think about of it.
granted i shouldn't be too surprised by the actions that you've taken.
it's exactly like it was last time.
how is it that you haven't changed or grown since high school?
i thought everyone changed a least a little bit?

it boggles my mind how you can spend four years of your life stuck in the same exact patterns.
how is it that so much time can go by and yet nothing about you has changed?
i feel as if i'm an entirely new person than who i was back in high school because i've learned from my past and all of my mistakes.
yet it's as if you haven't changed at all and i just can't wrap my head around how you've managed to do that.
it must take some effort to not change at all in such a long period of time.
i hope that one day you'll see the error of your ways,
just know that i won't be there this time when you decide you want to come back around.

objects.

the words you told me, keep ricocheting around in my head.
the same words that rolled off your tongue so effortlessly through your drunken lips, as if you'd rehearsed them.
you brag constantly about how brutally honest you are when you're plastered.
which thinking about now, makes it seem like a ruse to get me to believe it so i'd listen to anything you said.
were you ever honest with me?
i'd never be able to tell because your words and your actions never seemed to line up.
everything was always off.
the words said that first night make me rethink everything that's happened.
you told me that you never meant to hurt me, you hate hurting people and that's the last thing you'd ever want.
you sounded so sincere as if maybe you had feelings.
you said that you thought i was a good person.
anyone would be lucky to know me.
you said you were truly sorry and that you'd never let it happen again.
well here we are, you let it happen again.
i guess it was easy for you to apologize with the word "person" because i learned about your little category system soon after that conversation.
you have three distinct categories:
first: people/friends.

second: people you know/acquaintances.
and third, and this is my personal favorite: objects.
you told our dear friend that i was just an object in your mind.
you couldn't see me as a person. i was just something to entertain you.
an object.
it's easy to apologize to objects.
you had no problem building me up to tear me right back down because i wasn't a person to you.

i don't miss you anymore.

i've gotten better at not missing you.
i've only thought about you when i'm reading through my writing.
you hardly cross my mind anymore.
i'm thankful for that.
i finally feel like i'll be okay,
i tried to fill the void without you for so long and i think it's starting to work.
i think the thing i've thought about for so long was how you reacted to it all.
you were always very nonchalant when it came to people leaving you,
whereas i've always just expected people to leave,
even if that doesn't stop the ache when they're gone.
it's odd to think about.
i'm glad that i don't miss you anymore but that doesn't mean that i'm glad you left.
nothing will ever hurt me as much as that.
i know that it's my fault you're gone,
i messed up one too many times and you couldn't handle that.
i know that i'm the one who cut the ties so you couldn't talk to me anymore but you ghosted me long before then,
and i know that it's not fair of me to talk about you leaving me if i'm the one who pulled the final plug but you were gone long before then.

it makes me feel like i shouldn't be able to miss you because of that.
maybe i shouldn't.
everyone thought i was being overdramatic when it ended.
nobody understood why i reacted how i did but that's because i always kept what we did a secret.
i didn't want to tarnish your image in the eyes of our friends.
but you can only listen to "calm down it's not that serious" before you snap.
our friends know the things that transpired between us and i thank the stars above that nobody brought it up to you.
i cherish every moment i have with you and every memory that is engraved into my head.
even if you weren't always good to me i think you did your best and at the end of the day,
that's all that matters to me.
i don't miss you anymore and i've never felt so weightless.

part four: nightmares.

everything you read from here on out is pulled from dreams i have, things that instill fear in me, or simply things that are too scary for me to think about.

i've thought about splitting my works into parts but never quite figured out how to go about it or what i'd even want those parts to be. i've thought about it mostly as before and after the event and i came to the conclusion that isn't what i want.

i hope that you can make the connection between them all as well.

best wishes.

waiting for sleep.

i don't know if i can even sleep anymore.
i honestly can't remember the last time i could tell the difference between a dream and reality.
i wake up and i'm exhausted then i go to bed exhausted.
i close my eyes and i just lay there in bed for hours waiting for sleep to come to me.
i've tried everything.
i've taken melatonin, simply sleep, tylenol pm, and nyquil but nothing ever seems to help me.
do i even actually sleep once my eyes close or do i pretend that the thoughts running across my mind are my dreams?
am i ever actually awake or do i pretend that the dreams are my reality?
i can feel the scratchy sheets against my skin,
i can feel the soft cloudlike airiness of the pillow under my head,
i can feel the warmth of the blanket protecting me from the cold bitter air from the fan.
if i feel everything that must be a sign that i'm awake...right?
or does that simply mean i'm having a lucid dream and my mind is in control of it all?
night after night after night i lie awake in bed waiting and wishing for sleep's sweet embrace.
it's gotten to the point where i don't even bother trying to sleep anymore.

staying up until i crash at the end of the day should work, at least that's what i've been telling myself.
i think it might work.
i lie awake wondering, questioning, worrying.
why can i never seem to fall asleep?
why do all the days i've lived seem to just blur together?
why does it seem like i'm on autopilot all the time?
why is every day just a repeat of the one before it?
why isn't anything changing?

nightmares.

it's four in the morning and all i can think about is the horror that awaits me when i go to sleep.
which nightmare will be there tonight?
which face will i see when i close my eyes?
which old friend will haunt me tonight?
how could i bear to sleep when my dreams are cursed with the ghost of you?
i may never have another peaceful night's sleep for the rest of my life.
and it's all your fault.
i see people i can't even think about without my heart hurting.
i wish i could just have one night without any sort of dreams but i suppose that's asking for too much.
after a while, you start getting haunted by your mind.
you start digging up memories that you had buried so far into your brain.
your mind becomes your worst enemy.
i can't even trust myself.
i thought i was supposed to be on my own side,
how does that happen?
every day is a new battle.
every night is a war.
i usually always lose both without fail.
i've yet to win a single battle.
i have the battle scars to prove it.
sleeping used to be my safe haven,

and now the thought of sleep instills some sort of fear in me.
i can't imagine being that vulnerable around another person again.
i've got to go through a checklist before i can even think about closing my eyes.
i used to wait until the day to take naps and get a little bit of sleep but i can't even seem to do that anymore.
staying awake until i crash seems to, yet again, be my only option.

night.

i've always said that everything seems worse at night.
the mountains of despair and hopelessness always seem too high to climb in the dark of the night.
in the morning they'll seem like nothing more than a speed bump.
i've sat for hours and pondered on why that is.
why do things always seem to worsen tenfold when it's you by yourself in your head at night?
there's nothing you can do to convince yourself that you're overreacting,
you know deep down that your issue seems irrational but you can't talk yourself out of the nose dive solution that you've thought of.
too many times have i jumped from that mountain and regretted it the following morning because it wasn't that big of an issue and i made it something it wasn't.
try and think of all the things that have occurred in the dead of night that you convinced yourself that your world was ending.
now think of all the times it wasn't nearly as bad in the morning.
i try not to make big decisions at night simply for this reason.
if i make a choice that i can't have someone in my life anymore or i need to move or i need to hurt myself i have to force myself to hold off as long as i can to see how i feel about them in the morning.
otherwise, i'll regret it as soon as the sun breaks the horizon.

i know it's my own doing and that i should try harder to control myself but when it's just myself in the confines of my four walls,
it's nearly impossible to talk myself down from such heights.
i almost always have to distract myself with a movie or a show.
i stopped relying on people ages ago.
most of the time they won't pick up the phone for me.
and if they do nobody has ever been able to talk sense into me.
maybe this is something only i experience?
maybe i'm crazy and things just happen to me differently than they do for other people?
i hope someone out there thinks things are worse at night too.

up all night.

all i want is for the nightmares to stop.
every single time i close my eyes—without fail i have some horror awaiting me.
it's insane the amount of convincing i have to do before my body even considers shutting down.
it's been almost a year and a half since jacksonville and my body still is trying to protect me.
well by protecting me i mean that i'll have to stay up for hours on end to avoid someone touching me while i sleep.
i know that i'm safe in my room and the locked deadbolt is sure proof of that.
no matter how many times i turn the lock into place and push against it to ensure my safety,
it simply won't click in my mind that i'm safe when i close my eyes.
when i finally drift off to sleep it's never peaceful.
i wake up on average every three hours.
i wake up constantly during the night and i have nightmares daily.
for a while the nightmares were about the man in jacksonville,
then they were about him,
then they were about whatever my mind decides to scare me with that night.
i never take the peaceful nights for granted that i'm blessed with every once in a blue moon.
they never come when i need them though.

i have to wake up early for work and then the rest of the day i'm on the verge of sleeping.
now that i'm in bed however i can't seem to tip over the edge into a blissful slumber.
i'm so exhausted and there's nothing i can do to get myself to sleep.
i've tried everything and nothing seems to relieve me.
maybe i should give up and stay awake until i crash?
that's always worked in the past...
except for that time last week when i was up nearly twenty-four hours because the thought of sleeping terrified me to the point where i was running on adrenaline.
i can't stop yawning but i know for a fact that once my head hits the pillow again it'll be game over and i'll be begging mr. sandman to bring me a dream.
i don't care at this point whether i have a nightmare or not.
i'll welcome a nightmare.
please i'm so tired.
i just want to sleep.
i want to drift into unconsciousness for a while.
i can't stand being awake.
and i can't stand being asleep.
maybe there's simply no winning for me.

list of dates.
tw: self-harm.

tonight i found old notes and poems from 2016 tucked away in my laptop.
i wish i had found more of them.
in the mess of notes i found something that immediately brought tears to my eyes,
it was a list of dates and next to each date stood "x days clean".
it was a list i had made my junior year,
one of the first times my depression almost became too much to handle,
and the first few weeks i didn't make it more than three days without c*tting myself.
as the list got longer the days got farther apart,
twenty days since i last cracked,
forty-eight,
back to zero, what a failure i am.
then back to thirty,
hey now i'm at fifty-six and it seems like it's taken me a lifetime to get here.
you never realize how addicting hurting yourself is until you're trying to stop.
the days seemed to drag by so slowly when i was trying to stop and every day was such a battle.
and then when i failed and hit zero i didn't see the point in trying to stop because i always seemed to end up back there.
i made it all the way to ninety days.

i never recorded my hundredth day.
i don't think i've ever made it a full year.
a little over a year ago, i fell into that insane depression again and was right back where i started.
i couldn't stop,
i used to sit on my floor for hours and just tear myself apart until the tears in my eyes made it impossible to "safely" do it anymore.
then jacksonville happened, and i couldn't go more than an hour without hurting myself because i felt so disgusting and i wanted nothing more than to be dead.
nobody knows just how bad that was but i guess now everyone does because here we are.
there were so many nights i sat on my floor after jacksonville and almost just ended my pathetic life but i couldn't ever follow-through with that.
i'm glad that i didn't because a little over a year later i feel better than i ever have.
it's been a few months i think since the last time that cold metal blade has touched my skin and i no longer crave that burn.
things are finally starting to look up for me and it's crazy to think about.
every day seems to be a new adventure.
if you told me a year ago that i'd be here,
i never would have believed you.
i never thought that i could be happy in a million years and i truly believed that.

all that matters now is how far i've brought myself and how proud i am that despite it all i'm still here and kicking.
it's been such an uphill battle but i've reached the top and i think i'll stay a while.

take me under.

my whole life i've always felt off.
i've never been able to pinpoint why.
i'm starting to think i might feel things too much or feel them too deeply.
if you know "the secret life of bees" then you're familiar with the character May Boatwright.
in some way i've always identified with her because of how she feels so deeply.
my emotions consume me until i can't breathe, i don't think that's normal.
my chances of survival are slim to none.
they've almost dragged me under a few times these last few months.
things are supposed to get better so why do i just feel so much worse.
maybe i should just let them take me next time?
i haven't been truly happy in years,
i have fleeting moments at concerts or when i see my friends but it never lasts.
after the hell that was twenty nineteen, i don't know if i'll ever truly be happy again.
i just want a chance.
i have too many dark memories and thoughts.
maybe i'm meant to live like this forever.

my worst enemy is me.

i've been alone too much lately.
i don't like dealing with myself.
she's no fun.
she's cold and harsh.
i've been ripping myself apart trying to deal with her.
being alone with my thoughts is the hardest thing i've ever done?
why can't she just be nice to me?
maybe she doesn't like me just as much as i don't like her.
they always say that nobody could ever hate you as much as you hate yourself which i suppose is true.
i'm my own worst enemy.
the scariest realization is that she is me and i am her.
we are one.
i'm harsh on myself because i know i could be more than what i am.
i need to push myself.
i'm too scared because what if i fail?
my demons tell me i'm nothing and i'll never be more than that.
i'm delusional and i can't do anything.
maybe they're right.
why try?
the inner me needs to be defeated and i'm just too weak to do it.

escape.

she just wants to escape the monsters.
seems that every day there are more and more and she just can't escape them because they're surrounding her.
in her mind, they're telling her to do horrible things and commit horrible acts.
outside of her, they're whispering things into her ears making her collapse into tears at the worst possible times.
she's always wanting to cry no matter what is happening around her.
it feels like she's trapped with the walls closing in around her, they're suffocating her.
it feels like her brain is foggy and she can't focus or think clearly which is causing her to think irrationally.
she gives in to the monsters every time no matter how much she tries to fight it.
it's been a while since she's been able to think or even breathe clearly.
they don't look like monsters anymore,
they're more like long lost friends,
they look inviting.
she feels alone and scared when they leave her and it reminds her of how she felt when you left her.
a hollowed shell of the girl she once was.
nobody is noticing the changes in her,
she's no longer the positive bubbly girl that she once was.
she's turning into this lifeless zombie version of herself.

nobody seems to realize she's screaming for help.
she's pleading for it.
she just wants to escape these old friends.

alone.

i think i'm getting better at being by myself.
i really am!
at least that's what i tell myself when the room grows dark and the only one left dancing is me.
i figure if i tell myself that enough times then i'll start to believe it.
that's how it works right?
sunday was hard,
i didn't even realize the toll it took on me until everyone left and it was me alone in the room.
other than that i think i'm fine?
maybe i'm a bit lonely.
it doesn't help that he lives so far away although maybe that's for the best.
they can't see how clingy and annoying i really am.
i think i need to sit down and talk to myself.
i need to figure out why i hate being alone so much.
i think it has to do with the abandonment issues i've had all my life.
i need constant reassurance that they won't leave me and i need to have someone with me all the time.
everyone leaves me in the end,
i'd leave me too.

checklist.

i think the worst thing about my sleeping problems,
is that i know no matter how exhausted i am,
i will always be too scared to close my eyes and fall asleep.
i don't think there will ever be a time where i won't be scared
to fall asleep ever again.
i have to triple check my deadbolt and handle,
i have to turn on my string of lights above my bed and above
the desk,
i have to wrap the blankets around me as if i'm buried in,
and i have to hold onto my cold metal headboard
before i can even think about shutting my eyes.
it's so ridiculous that i have to have a system for going to bed,
i can't risk even the thought of you finding me in the middle of
the night.
i can't risk the thought of being exposed while i sleep.
i can't risk the thought of waking up and my mind playing
tricks on me.
there have been a few unfortunate times where
i've woken up and either thought i saw you sat at the foot of
my bed,
or i've woken up and thought i was back in that bed under you.
it's terrifying and it paralyzes me.
i'm so terrified all the time and there is nothing that i can do
about it because you've broken me.
it's like somehow you took every wire in my brain and you
rewired it to be in panic mode twenty-four hours of the day.

how did you manage to do that?
i'm never going to be able to wrap my head around why you did the things you did.
i don't think i want an answer to that question anyways.
i want you to get out of my head.
i want to feel safe.
i want to be myself again.
i want to be safe in my own skin.
in my own room.
in my own thoughts.
you have ruined everything i thought i was.

let me sleep.

i'm so insanely tired...
i just want to sleep.
however, sleep never seems to come.
at least not without a fight.
last month the biggest fight was dealing with images of self-harm behind my eyelids and the only way to get it to stop was to make those angry red marks appear.
now i'm sitting on my floor staring at the eight red lines on my leg and wondering how badly i must need to sleep if i was willing to go this far for it.
those thoughts are gone for now.
this month i'm stuck with your stupid laugh and you're dumb smile and the way your annoying eyes sparkle.
i don't know what's worse.
hurting myself or that.
i don't know how to get you out of my head.
i thought maybe if i saw a picture of you or i heard your voice in a video that it would stop.
nothing is helping and it's gotten worse.
now you're in my dreams and i can't get you out of my head.
i hope i haunt your dreams too, you asshole.
you don't get out of this so easily.
who the hell do you think you are?
i just want to sleep!
it's three-thirty in the morning.
see you in my dreams.

panic!

it's almost five in the morning and i think i'm losing my mind!
i shouldn't feel like this.
should i?
am i crazy?
is this normal?
am i overreacting?
i need to breathe.
i need to calm down.
what is going on with me?
i need to not be amber for a moment.
i need to step out of my life and think.
i need to not be me.
i can't do that though.
i can't just step outside of myself.
i can't just pause everything and take a moment.
life keeps going regardless of how bad you're spiraling.
it's one great big smack in the face,
"oh you need to calm down and sit? sike, get the hell up it's time to work."
trying to work through this is damn near impossible.
how am i meant to function?
my brain turns to mush.
the only thoughts i have are bad.
i think my body is trying to kill me.
i think my brain is trying to kill me.
i'm my own worst enemy.

evil within me.

you can feel like one of the tallest people in the world,
you can have friends that you see and talk to every day,
you can have a family that you know cares about you.
you can have friends on the internet that you know are always there for you no matter the time of day.
you can still feel so alone even knowing all of this and no matter what there's nothing you can do.
you can feel alone in a crowded room,
you can feel alone surrounded by friends,
you can feel alone in the arms of the person you love.
you can feel like a broken shell of a person,
you can feel like the most insignificant person on the planet.
no matter what you do to feel "happy",
you'll always have that voice in the back of your mind telling you that:
you're worthless,
you're invisible,
you mean nothing,
you do nothing but hurt people,
you don't deserve to live.
you'll find yourself agreeing with that voice that you once thought was a monster.
you'll start believing it,
you'll start enjoying its company,
you'll think of it as a friend.

pretty soon you'll find yourself calling out to it as you give up and your breathing slows and your heart stops.
as you're fading into the black you'll realize that voice in your head is you and you were your own worst enemy after all.
and the last thing your voice tells you is that it's won.
it took you down and there's no coming back.

tired.

i've spent so much time feeling like this,
like i'm nothing,
just a shell of a human.
i'm tired of feeling like this.
i'm tired of feeling like dust floating through the wind.
i'm tired of feeling like a memory in the minds of the people i love.
i want to feel like a permanent fixture,
i need the stability.
i want to feel like the sun,
i want to feel needed.
i want to feel like someone important.
i want to be remembered and have a legacy left behind.

i can't win.

what do you do when the thoughts in your head get so loud but none of them are saying anything worth hearing?
how do you get the voices in your head to quiet down?
i've tried too many times to quiet them with music,
i've covered my ears with a pillow,
i've put my fingers in my ears,
nothing i ever seem to do is enough.
i don't even know what triggered this tonight.
everything seems to be spinning and i can't stop it long enough to pinpoint the cause.
i need everything to stop.
i need the room to stand still.
i need the voices to stop.
i know it's not going to happen no matter how much i beg.
i've never been that lucky.
i have to try at sleep at some point to avoid going insane even though i already know that's how i'm going to end up.
i have to stay awake to avoid the nightmares.
i can't win.
usually i'd try and stay up until i hear the birds chirping but i'm so tired.
i miss my cats too.
i need to be in my room with smokey and luna.
i need to not be in my room but i know that if i start sleeping inside the house then i won't stop.
i won't be able to fall asleep outside again.

it happened last year,
i couldn't handle the nights by myself so i went in the house,
one night turned into a week,
a week turned into a month,
a month turned into over half the year.
i feel like i only just started sleeping out here again.
i can't ever seem to get it right.

goodbye?

driving too fast and caring too little.
i'm turning corners with reckless abandon.
no cares about if i live or if i die.
life is bland and i am unimportant.
death is unknown and exciting.
although i know i'd never pull that trigger because i'm too scared.
i'd probably just cry wolf until people gave up.
i haven't cried wolf yet.
i need a solid, foolproof plan before i do anything.
my original one still works i just have to be quick about it and turn the phone off before i reach the place so they can't track it.
no time to waste.
i guess i'd have all the time in the world though.
don't rush those final moments.
say your goodbyes.
make some calls.
make the call.
tell someone where to find you.
don't rot alone with the animals and bugs, that's no good to anyone.

wish.

wishes whispered on the cool breeze blowing through the trees,
making a mess of each perfect strand of hair upon your head.
wishes spent on dandelions in the green spring.
wishes we spent on things unattainable such as love or luck.
wishes spent as a child on horses, rockets, and toys!
those wonderful toys we saw on television as a kid!
the new red firetruck that lights up and has a siren!
the beautiful princess gown with the tiara and plastic slippers!
if only i had spent my wishes differently.
now those wishes on dandelions in the spring are spent on things other than those shiny new toys,
we're using them on cars, money, boys/girls, phones, and good grades.
the wonderfully fast shiny new car with the best engine.
the money that can pay for anything you'd ever wanted.
if i could make one single wish and have it come true at this point in time,
i think i would just wish for an adventure.
i wish i could travel far far away from here.
i think that's always a great option.
i would love to go to europe and see all the cheesy tourist attractions and take cheesy pictures.
i want to be able to take risks and have them work out.
i want to dive into the unknown and have it be okay.

lost cause.

i downloaded a dating app while we were on lockdown for shits and giggles.
i matched with a few really cool people!
one guy, in particular, was into basically everything i am and it seemed like a match made in heaven.
for the first time in a long time, i had hope about a relationship.
how silly of me.
we hung out once and i haven't heard from him since,
i'm not exactly surprised.
i'd probably ghost me too.
there are a few other people but they don't really hold a conversation they just send selfies back and forth and it's annoying because how the hell am i supposed to get to know you?
my sister met a guy on tinder a few days before i downloaded it and they're already official.
how the hell does she do it?
it's never been easy for me to talk to guys and it only got harder after everything because i can never know someone's true intentions.
i let people in and they just take everything i have from me and leave me broken on the floor.
i just get so SCARED!
being vulnerable is terrifying and i just can't risk letting someone in so they can tear me apart again.

i only have just begun to get myself back to where i was before then and it's taken so much time.
maybe i should stop trying to find someone until i find myself?
that seems to be the only logical thing that i can think of.
i just want to know how to stop being abandoned like this.
am i a lost cause?

talent trade.

the other day i was telling my friend how great his music was and that he was insanely talented,
he went on a tangent about how messed up his mind is and he feels like he traded his mental health for talent.
i told him that it usually goes hand in hand.
most artists who create masterpieces are tormented by the things in their minds.
i haven't heard from him in a few days and he hasn't been on social media.
i hope he's okay.
he wasn't in a good place the last time we spoke and that has me worried.
please be okay.

3:30 in the morning.

it's nearly three-thirty in the morning and once again i find myself waking up in a cold sweat panicking and in a fit of anxiety.
i didn't know where i was when i woke up.
this isn't the first time this has happened and i doubt it will be the last.
you have caused me a lifetime of horror and trauma and i know you don't care and you're never going to read this and that is so beyond okay with me.
it took me a moment to come to my senses and realize where i was.
i am safe.
i am in my room and i am safe.
i'm in my room and my door is locked and i am safe.
i'm in my room, my door is locked, i'm in my own bed, and i am safe.
i'm in my room, my door is locked, i'm in my own bed, there is nobody in my bed but me and i am safe.
these are the words i will repeat to myself for the rest of my life because of the trauma that you have inflicted on me.
you're not here and you never will be again and i am safe.
i don't understand how this happened.
i did everything right and i followed my checklist.
i held onto the cold metal railing to ground myself to my room when i woke up.

i left the lights above the bed on so when i woke up i could easily see where i was.
i tucked myself into the blanket burrito so tight so you wouldn't be able to get in and hurt me again.
i did everything right.
so why am i sitting here crying because i thought i was back in the bed in jacksonville?
why, after all of that and all of this time, do i still think you're going to find me?
i know with your connections it wouldn't be hard to find me at all.
i think that's what scares me the most,
i know that at any time you could easily find me.
you know my name and what town i live in and one simple question to the right person would have you at my doorstep in a heartbeat.
i'd like to think that after a year you wouldn't bother and you'd have your sights set on someone else.
please don't hurt her as you did to me.
it's been a year and a half almost and i'm still so scared to sleep because you haunt my every dream and you're here when i'm awake.
it's three-thirty in the morning and even though i know i'm safe in my bed i can still feel your filthy hands all over me and holding me down and i can't breathe.
it's three-thirty in the morning and the sudden overwhelming urge to run away has made itself known again,
tomorrow i have to get out of here.

i can't keep doing this i need to reset.
how do i escape the hell that is my own mind?
it's three-thirty in the morning and i'm forced to once again visit my exit strategy and wimp out.
nobody's going to be home it'd be perfect!
i need to be done with this.
i don't know how many more nights i can take of this.
it's inevitable.
i wasn't built to survive something this horrendous.
it's three-thirty in the morning and you're leading me, hand in mine, straight to my grave.

part five:
recovery.

for the first time, in such a long time, i'm starting to feel okay again.

i've started writing about it too which is probably one of the hardest things i've had to write about. anytime something good happens and i talk about it, it usually jinxes it so if i have a good day i avoid talking too much about it.

recovery isn't a linear path either. it's not good all of the time, there's still going to be bad days and i've included some pieces about those too because who would i be if i didn't show all of the parts to recovery?

hopefully one day you'll feel this good too.

que será.

don't let your brain get filled with what if's and might have been's.
don't let your mind run away with things you can't control.
there's always going to be an unexpected factor in your life that will mess everything up.
and that is okay.
you can't control everything.
you don't have to be in control all the time.
breathe.
it's okay.
your mind shall race about wonderland and the places you will go.
you will think about wonderland after it has fallen and the destruction left behind.
you might often think about things you can't change, but don't fret too much over them.
they're in your past and are history.
nothing you do or say will allow you to go back in time and change anything no matter how hard you try.
the days will come and go and soon enough they will be but a fleeting memory as you look back on your life.
this moment, in particular, will pass you without a moment's notice and will quickly become the newest memory in the archive of your brain.
you'll never be able to change what was but you can change what will be.

it's never too late to do something again in a different way.
every day is a new day, take it and make it something you're happy with.
make yourself proud.
you got this.

graduation.

i can probably qualify a few moments as the "greatest moment of my life (so far)".
graduating high school is probably the only one that stands out, i never thought i'd make it that far.
i remember walking into the coliseum for rehearsal and being so anxious, and we weren't even walking across the stage that day.
then the actual day came and my palms were so sweaty.
i wasn't sat near anyone i knew so that was terrifying because the only person i had to calm my nerves was myself and lord knows i'm not good at that.
i sat there as they read through the endless list of names and once they got to mine, it was like everything had stopped.
i could feel my heartbeat about to burst through my chest and my mouth was suddenly dry, "why didn't i bring any water or chapstick?"
my legs were shaking so fiercely i was nervous they were just going to fall off.
i stepped up onto the stage and shook hands with the longest line of people i'd ever seen and smiled at them so hard my cheeks hurt for days after that.
i remember almost falling as i stepped down from the stage.
it took everything in me to not run out the door after.
i waved to my parents after i sat back down and let out the air in my lungs i didn't even know i was holding.
i did it.

i made it through high school.
some of the hardest years of my life were over.
i was finally out.
all of the friends i had made and memories in the halls, cafeteria, breezeway...
all of it was done.
i would never sit in the bridge between the freshman hall and the 200 hall again in the morning with olivia and any other friends we happened to pick up that day.
sophia and i wouldn't walk to the car lot together after fourth period again.
i wouldn't get to eat with my best friends at lunch again.
i wouldn't be able to annoy mrs.shinn again in photography.
i wouldn't be able to hear insane stories from my forensics teacher again.
everything was coming to a close and i'd been so anxious about it that i forgot to enjoy the moments i had left.
after we left the coliseum my mom and dad took us home,
a few minutes later a small white car pulled up.
it was sophia and ashley, who are coincidentally two of my favorite people.
i don't think i would be who i am today without their jokes and enthusiasm.
then pulled up my mom's best friend with flowers for me and taking pictures.
i'll forever be grateful for that.
my neighbors were next, brad and sandra, they helped raise me from when i was just a baby.

they took care of me in the mornings when my mom was too sick to do it and they never once complained.
they're essentially my second parents and i owe them so much.
high school was really over and it was something i thought i'd never see.
high school was so rough i never thought i'd make it out alive.
june tenth, two thousand and seventeen was the greatest day of my life.

lessons.

i want to take all of my emotions and put them in a box much like pandora's,
i want to put it in that damn box and tie it with a cute bow.
i want to take that stupid box and set it adrift on the mississippi river.
i don't want to feel anything ever again for as long as i live.
i drown in my emotions all the time so it only makes sense that i drown them.
i want to be free.
letting go of the past isn't as easy as i thought it would be.
why did i even think this would be easy?
i've been doing everything.
i've been trying so hard.
i probably have more to learn from all of this but i'm so sick of the lessons.
i know they'll help me, in the long run, to stop myself from making these same mistakes.
i should do a little more self-reflecting and stop avoiding that because it's inevitable.
i have life lessons to learn.
i need to become a better person because who i am simply isn't cutting it anymore.
nobody wants to keep me around!
become the best version of myself...eventually.
put those lessons in a glass jar and dust it often so i never forget them.

never repeat those silly mistakes.
learn from them.
don't be a fool as i have been.

aim for the moon.

the phrase "aim for the moon, even if you miss you'll land upon the stars", always intrigued her.
she knew that the stars were millions upon millions of years old and the ones that are visible are either already dead or are dying.
the light that we see is from a star burning out.
did that mean that she's supposed to work until she's burned out and can't do anymore?
did that mean that everyone wanted her hopes and dreams to die out?
did they want themselves to outshine her until they outshone her?
did that mean they didn't really want her to make it?
do they expect her to fail and land somewhere equally as nice?
"you could've made it but you just missed the mark".
is that what she was to look forward to?
she figured she had the drive to make it to her end goal.
she figured maybe someone out there would support her dreams but the more the thinks about it maybe they're all just being nice to save face.
maybe nobody expects her to make it.
she'd have to try harder.
she'll make it to the moon even if she has to crawl.

lost.

you can easily get lost.
you can get lost in an idea, a person, or a place.
nobody ever expects to get lost it's just something that happens.
people often get lost while trying to escape their life.
that's how i got lost.
i was trying to run from myself and in return, i found the buildings lost to time.
the buildings are now thriving covered in vines, mold, creatures, and silence.
the buildings are chipped, crumbling, and deteriorating.
escaping can be hard,
it's been three years since i first got lost and i'm still trying to find my way back.
finding yourself is hard.
i think now more than ever i find myself hiding away in the depths of my own mind reminiscing of the times spent in those cold and quiet halls.
i want nothing more than to be back there.
the everyday stresses sometimes get too much for me and i just need an escape.
i've been running to the woods again in hopes of feeling something,
a month ago i ran to the mountains.
that always helps me to clear my mind.
i love getting away and being in nature and exploring,

i found new trails and spent 4 hours getting lost in the lush forest.
my footprints were the only sign that i had been there.
i took moments to sit and put my head back on the bench and just enjoy being there.
the sound of the creek and the chirping of birds while the wind blew through the trees will always be one of my favorite sounds.
will you get lost with me?
it's gotten lonely here.

the unknown.

i've spent so much time and energy on people who i know wouldn't even do the same for me.
i've consistently reached out the past few days and gotten nothing in return but i still see that you're posting on social media and i know that i'm not entitled to a reply and i'm not entitled to your time,
but just the other night wasn't it you who said that you were glad we reconnected and you weren't going to let me slip away again?
it's hard for me to believe that you truly feel that way when the way that you're acting now counteracts that so harshly.
i'm well aware i have a hard time figuring out people's intentions but i truly thought i knew yours like the back of my hand.
the whiplash you've given me is detrimental to my health.
i can't make sense of anything.
up is down and down is up when it comes to you.
god how could i be so dumb yet again.
no matter how many times i try i still get it wrong.
foolishly i reach out yet again and i pray that the outcome will be different.
did i jinx this by talking about it?
have the stars looked at me and they think that it's some sort of a game to do this to me again and again?
is this somehow my fault?
am i just not enough?

i just wish that things were different.
why can't something just go good for once.
you and i would be unstoppable and i think we both know it.
i think you're scared of what could be.
i am too.
the unknown will always be terrifying to me but i'm still foolish enough to want to take that leap.
i just wish i could find someone willing to jump with me.

happy birthday.

i realized tonight that your birthday is tomorrow.
shortly after realizing this, i sat down on my floor and started crying, i don't know what triggered that.
i'm debating if i should text you like i did last year, however, last year we were still in that odd limbo, we weren't really talking but i felt odd not saying it because you were such a staple in my life for so long it felt wrong to not wish you a happy birthday and that i hoped your year was a good one.
you deserved a good year.
it's odd to think about where we were this time last year versus this year.
i haven't spoken to you since my birthday.
you wished me a happy one and i said thanks and that was the end of it.
and for the next three hundred and sixty-five days you snuggled your way right back into my thoughts.
i went through my contacts and realized that i no longer have your number.
all i have is your facebook and i don't even know if you use that.
god i feel so dumb for even considering that.
but even if we aren't friends anymore i feel like that will only drive the nail into the coffin.
it's been over a year and i know you're no longer in my life and i'm able to talk about you and discuss you and i know that you're not coming back but something as simple as wishing an

old friend happy birthday just seems like something i have to do and it's so dumb because i know nothing will come from it and i don't owe you a single thing.
it's odd to think about how everything turned out with us.
a year apart and i feel like i've grown so much and learned so much and i hope you've changed too.
i hope this year is so good to you.
i hope this year is everything you never knew you needed.

one step forward, two steps back.

i've been talking about how i'm getting better but i don't know the extent of that.
mentally, sure, i'm doing better.
physically, yes, i suppose i am.
but i'm not sleeping again.
if i'm doing so well why am i not sleeping more than four hours a night?
why am i doing so poorly in that department?
i was doing so well and i was going to bed early and i was sleeping through the night and now i'm lucky if i only wake up twice during the four-hour span i'm asleep.
i don't know what changed...
now i'm staying up until six in the morning at least and eight-thirty at most.
i have work early in the day i can't afford to not be sleeping.
i don't know how to fix this.
any time i actually get some sleep it's nothing but nightmares and it's not even worth falling asleep.
why should i put myself through hell when i'm asleep on top of the demons i live with when i'm awake?
it doesn't make sense to me.
i just push through the waves of sleepiness until my body stops trying.
i know in the long run that's probably going to backfire on me but it's all i've got.
i just can't justify sleeping to myself.

other than the obvious mental changes that i can tell are happening i still feel exactly the same.
how does that happen?
i want so badly to be someone other than who i've been cursed with.
why did i have to be stuck like this?
i hope someday i'll be out of this weird sleep funk and not second guess sleeping.

phone calls.

as we sit on the phone talking,
i realize just how much i've missed you.
it feels like it's been ages since i've actually heard from you.
i've missed everything about you.
i've missed the way you laugh,
i've missed the way you get frustrated with your games.
i've missed sitting in mutual silence as we do our own thing.
i've even missed your voice.
our friendship has had many tests over time.
none more than the one we had when your sister and i had our falling out.
if i'm being honest,
as bad as this sounds,
i was more upset about the thought of losing you than i was about her.
despite everything, you'll always be one of my best friends.
i'm eternally grateful for you.
you've helped me through so many hardships,
i owe a lot to you.
i'd like to think that if we'd met in school we'd be even closer than we are now.
i wish we'd met through that rather than her.
if we're being honest i used to watch you from across the hall.
i might have had a small crush on you,
which you're painfully aware of now.

i think telling you that is easily one of the dumbest choices i ever made.
you could've lived your entire life without knowing that, it didn't change much.
which is fine i think i might be better like this actually.
i enjoy your company.
let's always stay this close.

doctor who.

i spend the majority of my time watching a show about an alien who can travel in time and space.
they always go somewhere amazing and have to save the day.
the doctor in their blue police box and their trusted sidekick.
what i would do to be whisked away in that blue box.
uprooted from everything.
thrown somewhere new to be an entirely new person.
i could completely change who i am, i could be someone strong and confident instead of the shy mousy girl i've become.
i think that would be magnificent.
saving people and learning so many new things.
the doctor and i against the world.
not even the scariest creature in the universe could tear us apart.
i think the tardis would like me too, i'd have some sort of likable quality about me that would be irresistible.
the last of their kind.
alone but never afraid.
incredibly brave.
i wish i was half the person they were.
i dream about that a lot.
a madman or woman in a blue box?
it sounds like a fun time to me.
i want to get away.
i'd gladly stow away.
i'll see you soon.

parts of me are parts of you.

it's been a year and a half without you,
and i'm still finding parts of you in me.
from the way i act,
to the way i talk,
to the way i dress,
even my silence reminds me of you sometimes.
when i get in my head and i start isolating somehow without fail my responses always end up as dry and pointless as yours were to me.
i can't let people in when i get like this because this isn't me, this is the version of me that you molded me to be.
i close myself off because that's what you taught me,
i couldn't even talk to you about my problems so i just closed off and isolated instead.
i had to learn to open up to people and realize that i wasn't bothering them by asking for help.
i hate how there's still a part of you with me even now.
i thought i did so well cleansing you out of my being,
i wanted to be rid of you.
i needed every bit of you gone.
i would say that i can't believe the impact you had on me but that would be a lie.
you molded me into who you wanted me to be and i listened because whenever i did something you didn't like you would scare me into listening by threatening to leave me and that's something that you knew i didn't want.

it took me so long to realize that it wasn't right and even longer for me to realize that i had to do what was best for me and remove myself from your hold.
i had to learn how to be myself again.
i had to figure out who i was before you and who i wanted to be after you,
the worst part of it was that nobody could relate to what i was going through and nobody could help me through it because nobody knew what i was going through.
i was so completely isolated and it was my own doing.
i can't blame anyone but myself because i brushed everyone else off for you.
i wanted to be there whenever you needed me and you needed me so much in our final months together so it just became easier for me to spend all my time and energy on you.
i didn't have any energy left for me.
how was i supposed to fix myself when i gave you every piece of me?
i gave you everything i had and then i had to start from the ground up to become who i am today.
i don't think anyone even noticed a change from who i was after you to who i am now.
it's taken a lot of self-reflecting and long nights but i've finally found who i am and i kinda like her.
it's odd to think about who i used to be.
the me i am today wouldn't have ever let you treat me like that.
i'm getting better at standing up for myself,
no thanks to you.

i stood down so many times because i was afraid of how you would react and now i know that the only person i should worry about is myself.
nothing will ever amount to the amount of love that i have for myself.
i've almost rid myself of you completely and i can't wait for the day that i look in the mirror and i don't see your ghost standing behind me.

dream catcher.

your dreams were banished into caves where they were forced to wither away until nothing but dust remained and you were too scared to go after them.
how could you forget the dreams that you've held tight since you were little?
how could you forget about the dream to be a marine biologist or a lawyer?
dreams were meant to be held tight and explored and chased.
you are supposed to run as fast as you can and reach the end goal of those dreams coming true.
sadly i've never been much of a runner and i'm always four feet behind where i should be and it's taking me ages to catch up.
i don't think i'll ever reach a point where i'll be happy with where i am in relation to these dreams.
it's been two years since i stopped chasing them and everything since then has seemed like a glitch.
nothing seems real and i'm not sure why they seem this way.
everything seems to blur together and i can't remember what day of the week it is or what today's date is.
i just know that i'm miserable...
why am i miserable again?
seems like i can't even keep that straight.
my dreams i was chasing seem so far out of reach and i don't know if it's even worth trying to catch up to them anymore.
i don't know how to even get back in that race.

i'm sure it's a long process and i need to put in work to make it happen and i know that i can do anything i put my mind to, the hard part is getting my mind set on them.
my adhd makes it hard to focus on things sometimes.
i either hyperfixate or i can't see what's in front of me.
that's how it's always been and i don't expect it to change for this.
maybe if i believed in myself a little bit more i wouldn't be in this predicament.
maybe if i had just tried harder the first time and not given up so easily i'd be doing better.
gotta get my head out of my ass and focus.
i'll make it there someday.
hopefully.

love myself.

for the first time in a very long time,
i feel great.
i don't know why this sudden change has happened and i don't want to question it and have it taken from me.
i weighed myself today which i almost never do because i hate the number that i see,
and can you imagine my surprise when i looked down and saw that i lost twenty pounds?
i don't know how or where it went because my body looks the same but my face looks slimmer and i know logically my face didn't lose that much.
since i've started being more open with my writing i've been feeling different too.
a great difference though.
i let go of weight on my shoulders that i wasn't even aware that i had on them.
almost every single one of my problems seems so small and minuscule now.
i can't picture myself being upset about things i used to lose sleep over on a regular basis.
i think most of it was all the weight i started carrying for him and the things we did but now that it's out there for everyone to know about i don't have this big secret i'm holding.
and i posted about the biggest tragedy in my life and that went well too so i don't have any more secrets.
you never realize how much of an effect those hold over you.

for the first time in such a long time...i don't hate who i've become.
after high school and after you left me and i didn't know who i was,
i spent so much time just trying to figure out who i was that i didn't realize i was so far from who i actually was.
how did i do that?
how did i let you mold me into someone i'm not?
i feel more like myself than i ever have,
and quite frankly i fucking love who she is.
and i did it all by myself.
without your opinion,
without your approval.
without anyone else helping me.
i did it all on my own and i'm so proud of myself.

Made in the USA
Columbia, SC
20 February 2022